Instant Vortex Dual Zone

Air Fryer Cookbook

1500 Days Quick, Savory and Nutritious Air Fryer Recipes for Your Family and Friends, Master the Art of Cooking Two Delicious Dishes Simultaneously

Courtney Donnelly

CONTENTS

Introduction 4

What is an Instant Vortex Dual Zone Air Fryer? 5
The Benefits of Using the Instant Vortex Dual Zone Air Fryer 6
How to Clean the Instant Vortex Dual Zone Air Fryer Properly? 7
Tips for Cooking on the Instant Vortex Dual Zone Air Fryer 8

Measurement Conversions 9

Breakfast & Snacks And Fries Recipes 11

Polenta Fries 12
Swede Fries 12
Plantain Fries 13
Oozing Baked Eggs 13
French Toast Slices 13
Courgette Fries 14
Monte Cristo Breakfast Sandwich 14
Muhammara 15
Hard Boiled Eggs Air Fryer Style 15
Tangy Breakfast Hash 15
Potato & Chorizo Frittata 16
Raspberry Breakfast Pockets 16
Pitta Pizza 17
European Pancakes 17
Wholegrain Pitta Chips 17
Avocado Fries 18
Mexican Breakfast Burritos 18
Bocconcini Balls 19
Your Favourite Breakfast Bacon 19
Easy Cheese & Bacon Toasties 19

Sauces & Snack And Appetiser Recipes 20

Popcorn Tofu 21
Snack Style Falafel 21
Mac & Cheese Bites 22
Garlic Pizza Toast 22
Mini Calzones 22
Thai Bites 23
Pasta Chips 23
Cheese Wontons 24
Onion Bahji 24
Chicken & Bacon Parcels 25
Asian Devilled Eggs 25
Stuffed Mushrooms 26
Waffle Fries 26
Tasty Pumpkin Seeds 26
Lumpia 27
Tortellini Bites 27
Corn Nuts 28
Onion Pakoda 28
Air-fried Pickles 29
Italian Rice Balls 29

Poultry Recipes 30

Chicken Milanese 31
Air Fryer Chicken Thigh Schnitzel 31
Thai Turkey Burgers 32
Buffalo Wings 32
Olive Stained Turkey Breast 33
Healthy Bang Bang Chicken 33
Chicken Parmesan With Marinara Sauce 34
Chicken Tikka Masala 34
Charred Chicken Breasts 35
Pizza Chicken Nuggets 35
Chicken Fried Rice 36
Nashville Chicken 36
Chicken And Cheese Chimichangas 37
Pepper & Lemon Chicken Wings 37
Turkey Cutlets In Mushroom Sauce 38
Chicken Kiev 38
Quick Chicken Nuggets 39
Honey Cajun Chicken Thighs 39
Chicken & Potatoes 40
Orange Chicken 40

Beef & Lamb And Pork Recipes 41

Old Fashioned Steak 42
Roast Beef 42
Tahini Beef Bites 43
Beef Satay 43
Pizza Dogs 44
Pork Taquitos 44
Pulled Pork, Bacon, And Cheese Sliders 45
Taco Lasagne Pie 45
Asparagus & Steak Parcels 46
Beef Bulgogi Burgers 46
Meatballs In Tomato Sauce 47
Sausage Burritos 47
Pork Schnitzel 48
Cheesy Meatballs 48
Tender Ham Steaks 49
Pork Chops With Honey 49
Parmesan Crusted Pork Chops 50
Pork Chilli Cheese Dogs 50
Hamburgers 51
Pork Chops With Raspberry And Balsamic 51

Fish & Seafood Recipes 52

Parmesan-coated Fish Fingers 53
Lobster Tails 53
Honey Sriracha Salmon 54
Shrimp With Yum Yum Sauce 54
Crispy Nacho Prawns 54
Store-cupboard Fishcakes 55
Garlic Tilapia 55
Traditional Fish And Chips 56
Fish In Parchment Paper 56
Crunchy Fish 57
Fish Taco Cauliflower Rice Bowls 57
Garlic Butter Salmon 58
Cod Nuggets 58
Fish In Foil 58
Copycat Fish Fingers 59
Maine Seafood 59
Shrimp Wrapped With Bacon 60
Thai Salmon Patties 60
Air Fried Scallops 61
Oat & Parmesan Crusted Fish Fillets 61

Vegetarian & Vegan Recipes 62

Veggie Lasagne 63
Courgette Meatballs 63
Ratatouille 64
Two-step Pizza 64
Stuffed Peppers 65
Vegetarian "chicken" Tenders 65
Air Fryer Cheese Sandwich 66
Air-fried Artichoke Hearts 66
Baked Feta, Tomato & Garlic Pasta 67
Satay Tofu Skewers 67
Macaroni & Cheese Quiche 68
Mini Quiche 68
Roasted Vegetable Pasta 69
Baked Aubergine Slices With Yogurt Dressing 69
Vegan Fried Ravioli 70
Artichoke Crostini 70
Falafel Burgers 71
Artichoke Pasta 71

Aubergine Parmigiana.. 72
Crispy Potato Peels 72

Side Dishes Recipes 73

Crispy Broccoli 74
Cauliflower With Hot Sauce And Blue Cheese Sauce 74
Asparagus Spears 75
Mediterranean Vegetables 75
Crispy Cinnamon French Toast.............................. 75
Butternut Squash 76
Garlic And Parsley Potatoes.................................... 76
Sweet And Sticky Parsnips And Carrots 76
Butternut Squash Fries 77
Celery Root Fries 77
Carrot & Parmesan Chips 77
Yorkshire Puddings 78
Aubergine Parmesan 78
Onion Rings 79
Grilled Bacon And Cheese 79
Roasted Okra 80
Ranch-style Potatoes 80
Zingy Brussels Sprouts 80
Homemade Croquettes 81
Roasted Brussels Sprouts 81

Desserts Recipes 82

Shortbread Cookies 83
Blueberry Muffins 83
Cinnamon-maple Pineapple Kebabs 83
New York Cheesecake 84
Granola Bars 84
Pop Tarts 85
Apple And Cinnamon Empanadas 85
Fruit Crumble 86
Chocolate Dipped Biscuits 86
Pecan & Molasses Flapjack 86
S'mores 87
Apple And Cinnamon Puff Pastry Pies 87
Tasty Cannoli 88
Chocolate Mug Cake 88
Cinnamon Biscuit Bites 89
Apple Pie 89
Breakfast Muffins 90
Granola 90
Chocolate And Berry Pop Tarts 91
Apple Fritters 91

Appendix : Recipes Index 92

INTRODUCTION

The Instant Vortex Dual Zone Air Fryer Cookbook, a collection of delicious and easy-to-make recipes that are perfect for the Instant Vortex Dual Zone Air Fryer. My name is Courtney Donnelly, and I am a passionate home cook and food blogger. I have always loved experimenting with new recipes and sharing my creations with others. When I discovered the Instant Vortex Dual Zone Air Fryer, I was immediately hooked. This amazing appliance makes it easy to cook healthy and delicious meals quickly and easily, which is why I decided to write this cookbook.

As a busy mom of three, I know how difficult it can be to find the time to cook healthy meals for my family. That's why I love the Instant Vortex Dual Zone Air Fryer. It allows me to prepare delicious meals in just minutes, without sacrificing flavor or nutrition. I started experimenting with different recipes and soon discovered that the possibilities were endless. From crispy chicken wings to tender roasted vegetables, the Instant Vortex Dual Zone Air Fryer can do it all.

In this cookbook, I have compiled some of my favorite recipes for the Instant Vortex Dual Zone Air Fryer. These recipes are easy to follow and use simple, wholesome ingredients that you probably already have in your pantry. Whether you're a seasoned home cook or a beginner, you'll find something in this cookbook that you'll love.

All of the recipes in this cookbook have been tested and perfected to ensure that they work perfectly with the Instant Vortex Dual Zone Air Fryer. I have also included cooking tips and tricks to help you get the most out of your appliance.

In addition to the recipes, the Instant Vortex Dual Zone Air Fryer Cookbook also includes a brief introduction to the Instant Vortex Dual Zone Air Fryer, as well as tips for cleaning and maintaining your appliance. This information will help you get the most out of your appliance and ensure that it lasts for years to come.

Overall, the Instant Vortex Dual Zone Air Fryer Cookbook is the ultimate guide to cooking with the Instant Vortex Dual Zone Air Fryer. Whether you're a busy parent, a health-conscious individual, or just someone who loves good food, this cookbook has something for everyone. With easy-to-follow recipes and helpful tips, you'll be cooking up delicious and healthy meals in no time. So what are you waiting for? Grab your copy today and get cooking!

What is an Instant Vortex Dual Zone Air Fryer?

The Instant Vortex Dual Zone Air Fryer is a kitchen appliance that uses hot air to cook food quickly and evenly. It is a versatile appliance that can be used for a wide variety of cooking tasks, including air frying, roasting, baking, reheating, and dehydrating. The Instant Vortex Dual Zone Air Fryer is designed to be easy to use, with intuitive controls and pre-programmed settings for different types of food. It also features a dual-zone cooking system that allows you to cook two different foods at the same time, without mixing flavors or aromas.

One of the main features of the Instant Vortex Dual Zone Air Fryer is its air frying capability. Air frying is a healthier alternative to deep frying, as it uses hot air to cook food instead of oil. The Instant Vortex Dual Zone Air Fryer uses a powerful fan to circulate hot air around the food, cooking it to a crispy and golden brown finish. It's perfect for cooking crispy chicken wings, French fries, onion rings, and other fried foods.

In addition to air frying, the Instant Vortex Dual Zone Air Fryer can also be used for roasting and baking. It features a spacious interior that can accommodate large items such as whole chickens, roasts, and casseroles. It also has pre-programmed settings for baking cakes, muffins, and other desserts.

The Instant Vortex Dual Zone Air Fryer is designed with convenience in mind. It features a digital control panel that allows you to easily set the cooking time and temperature. It also has a built-in timer and automatic shut-off feature, so you can set it and forget it. The appliance is also easy to clean, with a removable and dishwasher-safe cooking basket and drip tray.

One of the unique features of the Instant Vortex Dual Zone Air Fryer is its dual-zone cooking system. This allows you to cook two different foods at the same time, without mixing flavors or aromas. Each zone has its own cooking basket and temperature control, so you can cook two different foods with different cooking times and temperatures.

The Instant Vortex Dual Zone Air Fryer is a versatile and convenient appliance that can make cooking easier and more enjoyable. It's perfect for busy families who want to cook healthy and delicious meals quickly and easily. With its air frying, roasting, and baking capabilities, as well as its dual-zone cooking system, the Instant Vortex Dual Zone Air Fryer is sure to become a staple in any kitchen.

The Benefits of Using the Instant Vortex Dual Zone Air Fryer

1. Healthier Cooking

One of the main benefits of using the Instant Vortex Dual Zone Air Fryer is that it allows you to cook food in a healthier way. Instead of deep frying food in oil, the air fryer uses hot air to cook food to a crispy and golden brown finish. This means that you can enjoy crispy and delicious food without the added calories and fat.

2. Versatility

The Instant Vortex Dual Zone Air Fryer is a versatile appliance that can be used for a wide range of cooking tasks, including air frying, roasting, baking, reheating, and dehydrating. This means that you can use it to cook everything from crispy chicken wings to tender roasted vegetables and even homemade bread.

3. Time-Saving

The Instant Vortex Dual Zone Air Fryer is designed to cook food quickly and evenly. This means that you can cook food in less time than traditional cooking methods, which is perfect for busy families or anyone who wants to save time in the kitchen.

4. Easy to Use

The Instant Vortex Dual Zone Air Fryer is designed to be easy to use, with intuitive controls and pre-programmed settings for different types of food. This means that you don't need to be a professional chef to use it, and you can start cooking delicious meals right away.

5. Dual-Zone Cooking

The Instant Vortex Dual Zone Air Fryer features a dual-zone cooking system that allows you to cook two different foods at the same time, without mixing flavors or aromas. Each zone has its own cooking basket and temperature control, so you can cook two different foods with different cooking times and temperatures.

6. Easy to Clean

The Instant Vortex Dual Zone Air Fryer is easy to clean, with a removable and dishwasher-safe cooking basket and drip tray. This means that you can clean up quickly and easily after cooking, without having to spend time scrubbing the appliance.

7. Energy Efficient

The Instant Vortex Dual Zone Air Fryer is an energy-efficient appliance that uses less energy than traditional cooking methods. This means that you can save money on your energy bills while still enjoying delicious and healthy food.

Overall, the Instant Vortex Dual Zone Air Fryer is a versatile and convenient appliance that offers a range of benefits for home cooks. Whether you're looking to cook healthier meals, save time in the kitchen, or simply enjoy delicious and crispy food, the Instant Vortex Dual Zone Air Fryer is a great choice.

How to Clean the Instant Vortex Dual Zone Air Fryer Properly?

Properly cleaning your Instant Vortex Dual Zone Air Fryer after each use is important to ensure that it continues to function properly and to prevent any potential health hazards. Here's how to clean your Instant Vortex Dual Zone Air Fryer properly:

1. Unplug the appliance

Before cleaning, make sure that the Instant Vortex Dual Zone Air Fryer is unplugged and has cooled down completely.

2. Remove the cooking basket

Remove the cooking basket from the appliance and set it aside.

3. Clean the drip tray

Remove the drip tray from the appliance and wash it with warm, soapy water. Rinse it thoroughly and dry it with a clean cloth or paper towel.

4. Clean the cooking basket

The cooking basket can be washed by hand with warm, soapy water, or it can be placed in the dishwasher. If washing by hand, use a non-abrasive sponge or brush to avoid scratching the non-stick surface. Rinse the basket thoroughly and dry it with a clean cloth or paper towel.

5. Clean the interior

Wipe down the interior of the appliance with a damp cloth or sponge. Be careful not to get any water or cleaning solution in the heating element or other electrical components.

6. Clean the exterior

Wipe down the exterior of the appliance with a damp cloth or sponge. Use a non-abrasive cleaner to remove any stubborn stains or residue.

7. Reassemble the appliance

Once all the parts are clean and dry, reassemble the Instant Vortex Dual Zone Air Fryer and store it in a dry place.

It is important to clean the Instant Vortex Dual Zone Air Fryer after each use to prevent any buildup of grease, food particles, or bacteria. Regular cleaning will also help to extend the life of your appliance and ensure that it continues to function properly.

Tips for Cooking on the Instant Vortex Dual Zone Air Fryer

Preheat the appliance: Preheating the Instant Vortex Dual Zone Air Fryer before cooking will ensure that the food cooks evenly and to the desired temperature.

1. Use the right temperature: The Instant Vortex Dual Zone Air Fryer has pre-programmed settings for different types of food, but it's important to adjust the temperature and cooking time based on the specific recipe you're using. Follow the recipe instructions for best results.

2. Don't overcrowd the basket: It's important not to overcrowd the cooking basket, as this can prevent the food from cooking evenly. Leave enough space between the food items to allow hot air to circulate freely.

3. Shake the basket: Shake the cooking basket occasionally during cooking to ensure that the food cooks evenly on all sides.

4. Use cooking spray: Using a cooking spray such as olive oil or vegetable oil can help to prevent the food from sticking to the cooking basket and can also help to achieve a crispier texture.

5. Season the food: Adding seasoning or spices to the food before cooking can enhance the flavor and make it more delicious.

6. Experiment with different recipes: The Instant Vortex Dual Zone Air Fryer is a versatile appliance that can be used for a wide range of recipes. Experiment with different recipes to find your favorite dishes.

By following these tips and tricks, you can get the most out of your Instant Vortex Dual Zone Air Fryer and cook delicious and healthy meals in no time.

Measurement Conversions

BASIC KITCHEN CONVERSIONS & EQUIVALENTS

DRY MEASUREMENTS CONVERSION CHART

3 TEASPOONS = 1 TABLESPOON = 1/16 CUP

6 TEASPOONS = 2 TABLESPOONS = 1/8 CUP

12 TEASPOONS = 4 TABLESPOONS = 1/4 CUP

24 TEASPOONS = 8 TABLESPOONS = 1/2 CUP

36 TEASPOONS = 12 TABLESPOONS = 3/4 CUP

48 TEASPOONS = 16 TABLESPOONS = 1 CUP

METRIC TO US COOKING CONVERSIONS

OVEN TEMPERATURES

120 °C = 250 °F

160 °C = 320 °F

180° C = 350 °F

205 °C = 400 °F

220 °C = 425 °F

LIQUID MEASUREMENTS CONVERSION CHART

8 FLUID OUNCES = 1 CUP = 1/2 PINT = 1/4 QUART

16 FLUID OUNCES = 2 CUPS = 1 PINT = 1/2 QUART

32 FLUID OUNCES = 4 CUPS = 2 PINTS = 1 QUART = 1/4 GALLON

128 FLUID OUNCES = 16 CUPS = 8 PINTS = 4 QUARTS = 1 GALLON

BAKING IN GRAMS

1 CUP FLOUR = 140 GRAMS

1 CUP SUGAR = 150 GRAMS

1 CUP POWDERED SUGAR = 160 GRAMS

1 CUP HEAVY CREAM = 235 GRAMS

VOLUME

1 MILLILITER = 1/5 TEASPOON

5 ML = 1 TEASPOON

15 ML = 1 TABLESPOON

240 ML = 1 CUP OR 8 FLUID OUNCES

1 LITER = 34 FL. OUNCES

WEIGHT

1 GRAM = .035 OUNCES

100 GRAMS = 3.5 OUNCES

500 GRAMS = 1.1 POUNDS

1 KILOGRAM = 35 OUNCES

US TO METRIC COOKING CONVERSIONS

1/5 TSP = 1 ML

1 TSP = 5 ML

1 TBSP = 15 ML

1 FL OUNCE = 30 ML

1 CUP = 237 ML

1 PINT (2 CUPS) = 473 ML

1 QUART (4 CUPS) = .95 LITER

1 GALLON (16 CUPS) = 3.8 LITERS

1 OZ = 28 GRAMS

1 POUND = 454 GRAMS

BUTTER

1 CUP BUTTER = 2 STICKS = 8 OUNCES = 230 GRAMS = 8 TABLESPOONS

WHAT DOES 1 CUP EQUAL

1 CUP = 8 FLUID OUNCES

1 CUP = 16 TABLESPOONS

1 CUP = 48 TEASPOONS

1 CUP = 1/2 PINT

1 CUP = 1/4 QUART

1 CUP = 1/16 GALLON

1 CUP = 240 ML

BAKING PAN CONVERSIONS

1 CUP ALL-PURPOSE FLOUR = 4.5 OZ

1 CUP ROLLED OATS = 3 OZ 1 LARGE EGG = 1.7 OZ

1 CUP BUTTER = 8 OZ 1 CUP MILK = 8 OZ

1 CUP HEAVY CREAM = 8.4 OZ

1 CUP GRANULATED SUGAR = 7.1 OZ

1 CUP PACKED BROWN SUGAR = 7.75 OZ

1 CUP VEGETABLE OIL = 7.7 OZ

1 CUP UNSIFTED POWDERED SUGAR = 4.4 OZ

BAKING PAN CONVERSIONS

9-INCH ROUND CAKE PAN = 12 CUPS

10-INCH TUBE PAN =16 CUPS

11-INCH BUNDT PAN = 12 CUPS

9-INCH SPRINGFORM PAN = 10 CUPS

9 X 5 INCH LOAF PAN = 8 CUPS

9-INCH SQUARE PAN = 8 CUPS

Breakfast & Snacks And Fries Recipes

Polenta Fries

Servings: 6
Cooking Time:xx

Ingredients:
- 800 ml/scant 3½ cups water
- 1½ vegetable stock cubes
- ¾ teaspoon dried oregano
- ¾ teaspoon freshly ground black pepper
- 200 g/1⅓ cups quick-cook polenta/cornmeal
- 2 teaspoons olive oil
- 55 g/6 tablespoons plain/all-purpose flour (gluten-free if you wish)
- garlic mayonnaise, to serve

Directions:
1. Bring the water and stock cubes to the boil in a saucepan with the oregano and black pepper. Stir in the polenta/cornmeal and continue to stir until the mixture becomes significantly more solid and is hard to stir – this should take about 5–6 minutes.
2. Grease a 15 x 15-cm/6 x 6-in. baking pan with some of the olive oil. Tip the polenta into the baking pan, smoothing down with the back of a wet spoon. Leave to cool at room temperature for about 30 minutes, then pop into the fridge for at least an hour.
3. Remove the polenta from the fridge and carefully tip out onto a chopping board. Slice the polenta into fingers 7.5 x 1 x 2 cm/3 x ½ x ¾ in. Roll the polenta fingers in the flour, then spray or drizzle the remaining olive oil over the fingers.
4. Preheat the air-fryer to 200°C/400°F.
5. Lay the fingers apart from one another in a single layer in the preheated air-fryer (you may need to cook these in batches, depending on the size of your air-fryer). Air-fry for 9 minutes, turning once halfway through cooking. Serve immediately with garlic mayonnaise.

Swede Fries

Servings: 4
Cooking Time:xx

Ingredients:
- 1 medium swede/rutabaga
- ½ teaspoon salt
- ½ teaspoon freshly ground black pepper
- 1½ teaspoons dried thyme
- 1 tablespoon olive oil

Directions:
1. Preheat the air-fryer to 160°C/325°F.
2. Peel the swede/rutabaga and slice into fries about 6 x 1 cm/2½ x ½ in., then toss the fries in the salt, pepper, thyme and oil, making sure every fry is coated.
3. Tip into the preheated air-fryer in a single layer (you may need to cook them in two batches, depending on the size of your air-fryer) and air-fry for 15 minutes, shaking the drawer halfway through. Then increase the temperature to 180°C/350°F and cook for a further 5 minutes. Serve immediately.

Plantain Fries

Servings: 2
Cooking Time:xx

Ingredients:

- 1 ripe plantain (yellow and brown outside skin)
- 1 teaspoon olive oil
- ¼ teaspoon salt

Directions:

1. Preheat the air-fryer to 180ºC/350ºF.
2. Peel the plantain and slice into fries about 6 x 1 cm/2½ x ½ in. Toss the fries in oil and salt, making sure every fry is coated.
3. Tip into the preheated air-fryer in a single layer (you may need to cook them in two batches, depending on the size of your air-fryer) and air-fry for 13–14 minutes until brown on the outside and soft on the inside. Serve immediately.

Oozing Baked Eggs

Servings: 2
Cooking Time:xx

Ingredients:

- 4 eggs
- 140g smoked gouda cheese, cut into small pieces
- Salt and pepper to taste

Directions:

1. You will need two ramekin dishes and spray each one before using
2. Crack two eggs into each ramekin dish
3. Add half of the Gouda cheese to each dish
4. Season and place into the air fryer
5. Cook at 350ºC for 15 minutes, until the eggs are cooked as you like them

French Toast Slices

Servings: 1
Cooking Time:xx

Ingredients:

- 2 eggs
- 5 slices sandwich bread
- 100ml milk
- 2 tbsp flour
- 3 tbsp sugar
- 1 tsp ground cinnamon
- 1/2 tsp vanilla extract
- Pinch of salt

Directions:

1. Preheat your air fryer to 220ºC
2. Take your bread and cut it into three pieces of the same size
3. Take a mixing bowl and combine the other ingredients until smooth
4. Dip the bread into the mixture, coating evenly
5. Take a piece of parchment paper and lay it inside the air fryer
6. Arrange the bread on the parchment paper in one layer
7. Cook for 5 minutes
8. Turn and cook for another 5 minutes

Courgette Fries

Servings: 2
Cooking Time:xx

Ingredients:

- 1 courgette/zucchini
- 3 tablespoons plain/all-purpose flour (gluten-free if you wish)
- ¼ teaspoon salt
- ¼ teaspoon freshly ground black pepper
- 60 g/¾ cup dried breadcrumbs (gluten-free if you wish; see page 9)
- 1 teaspoon dried oregano
- 20 g/¼ cup finely grated Parmesan
- 1 egg, beaten

Directions:

1. Preheat the air-fryer to 180°C/350°F.
2. Slice the courgette/zucchini into fries about 1.5 x 1.5 x 5 cm/⅝ x ⅝ x 2 in.
3. Season the flour with salt and pepper. Combine the breadcrumbs with the oregano and Parmesan.
4. Dip the courgettes/zucchini in the flour (shaking off any excess flour), then the egg, then the seasoned breadcrumbs.
5. Add the fries to the preheated air-fryer and air-fry for 15 minutes. They should be crispy on the outside but soft on the inside. Serve immediately.

Monte Cristo Breakfast Sandwich

Servings: 4
Cooking Time:xx

Ingredients:

- 1 egg
- 2 slices of sandwich bread
- 1/4 tsp vanilla extract
- 4 slices of sliced Swiss cheese
- 4 slices of sliced deli ham
- 4 slices of sliced turkey
- 1 tsp melted butter
- Powdered sugar for serving

Directions:

1. In a small bowl, mix together the egg and vanilla extract, combining well
2. Take your bread and assemble your sandwich, starting with a slice of cheese, then the ham, turkey, and then another slice of the cheese, with the other slice of bread on the top
3. Compress the sandwich a little, so it cooks better
4. Take a piece of cooking foil and brush over it with the butter
5. Take your sandwich and dip each side into the egg mixture, leaving it to one side for around half a minute
6. Place the sandwich on the foil and place it inside your fryer
7. Cook at 200°C for around 10 minutes, before turning the sandwich over and cooking for another 8 minutes
8. Transfer your sandwich onto a plate and sprinkle with a little powdered sugar

Muhammara

Servings: 4
Cooking Time:xx

Ingredients:

- 4 romano peppers
- 4 tablespoons olive oil
- 100 g/1 cup walnuts
- 90 g/1 heaped cup dried breadcrumbs (see page 9)
- 1 teaspoon cumin
- 2 tablespoons pomegranate molasses
- freshly squeezed juice of ½ a lemon
- ½ teaspoon chilli/chili salt (or salt and some chilli/hot red pepper flakes combined)
- fresh pomegranate seeds, to serve

Directions:

1. Preheat the air-fryer to 180°C/350°F.
2. Rub the peppers with ½ teaspoon of the olive oil. Add the peppers to the preheated air-fryer and air-fry for 8 minutes.
3. Meanwhile, lightly toast the walnuts by tossing them in a shallow pan over a medium heat for 3–5 minutes. Allow to cool, then grind the walnuts in a food processor. Once the peppers are cooked, chop off the tops and discard most of the seeds. Add to the food processor with all other ingredients. Process until smooth. Allow to cool in the fridge, then serve the dip with pomegranate seeds on top.

Hard Boiled Eggs Air Fryer Style

Servings: 2
Cooking Time:xx

Ingredients:

- 4 large eggs
- 1 tsp cayenne pepper
- Salt and pepper for seasoning

Directions:

1. Preheat the air fryer to 220°C
2. Take a wire rack and place inside the air fryer
3. Lay the eggs on the rack
4. Cook for between 15-17 minutes, depending upon how you like your eggs
5. Remove from the fryer and place in a bowl of cold water for around 5 minutes
6. Peel and season with the cayenne and the salt and pepper

Tangy Breakfast Hash

Servings: 6
Cooking Time:xx

Ingredients:

- 2 tbsp olive oil
- 2 sweet potatoes, cut into cubes
- 1 tbsp smoked paprika
- 1 tsp salt
- 1 tsp black pepper
- 2 slices of bacon, cut into small pieces

Directions:

1. Preheat your air fryer to 200°C
2. Pour the olive oil into a large mixing bowl
3. Add the bacon, seasonings, potatoes and toss to evenly coat
4. Transfer the mixture into the air fryer and cook for 12-16 minutes
5. Stir after 10 minutes and continue to stir periodically for another 5 minutes

Potato & Chorizo Frittata

Servings: 2
Cooking Time:xx

Ingredients:
- 3 eggs
- 1 sliced chorizo sausage
- 1 potato, boiled and cubed
- 50g feta cheese
- 50g frozen sweetcorn
- A pinch of salt
- 1 tbsp olive oil

Directions:
1. Add a little olive oil to the frying basket
2. Add the corn, potato, and sliced chorizo to the basket
3. Cook at 180ºC until the sausage is a little brown
4. In a small bowl, beat together the eggs with a little seasoning
5. Pour the eggs into the pan
6. Crumble the feta on top
7. Cook for 5 minutes
8. Remove and serve in slices

Raspberry Breakfast Pockets

Servings: 1
Cooking Time:xx

Ingredients:
- 2 slices of sandwich bread
- 1 tbsp soft cream cheese
- 1 tbsp raspberry jam
- 1 tbsp milk
- 1 egg

Directions:
1. Take one slice of the bread and add one tablespoon of jam into the middle
2. Take the second slice and add the cream cheese into the middle
3. Using a blunt knife, spread the jam and the cheese across the bread, but don't go to the outer edges
4. Take a small bowl and whisk the eggs and the milk together
5. Set your fryer to 190ºC and spray with a little oil
6. Dip your sandwich into the egg and arrange inside your fryer
7. Cook for 5 minutes on the first side, turn and cook for another 2 minutes

Pitta Pizza

Servings: 2
Cooking Time:xx

Ingredients:
- 2 round wholemeal pitta breads
- 3 tablespoons passata/strained tomatoes
- 4 tablespoons grated mozzarella
- 1 teaspoon dried oregano
- 1 teaspoon olive oil
- basil leaves, to serve

Directions:
1. Preheat the air-fryer to 200ºC/400ºF.
2. Pop the pittas into the preheated air-fryer and air-fry for 1 minute.
3. Remove the pittas from the air-fryer and spread a layer of the passata/strained tomatoes on the pittas, then scatter over the mozzarella, oregano and oil. Return to the air-fryer and air-fry for a further 4 minutes. Scatter over the basil leaves and serve immediately.

European Pancakes

Servings: 5
Cooking Time:xx

Ingredients:
- 3 large eggs
- 130g flour
- 140ml whole milk
- 2 tbsp unsweetened apple sauce
- A pinch of salt

Directions:
1. Set your fryer to 200ºC and add five ramekins inside to heat up
2. Place all your ingredients inside a blender to combine
3. Spray the ramekins with a little cooking spray
4. Pour the batter into the ramekins carefully
5. Fry for between 6-8 minutes, depending on your preference
6. Serve with your favourite toppings

Wholegrain Pitta Chips

Servings: 2
Cooking Time:xx

Ingredients:
- 2 round wholegrain pittas, chopped into quarters
- 1 teaspoon olive oil
- ½ teaspoon garlic salt

Directions:
1. Preheat the air-fryer to 180ºC/350ºF.
2. Spray or brush each pitta quarter with olive oil and sprinkle with garlic salt. Place in the preheated air-fryer and air-fry for 4 minutes, turning halfway through cooking. Serve immediately.

Avocado Fries

Servings: 2
Cooking Time:xx

Ingredients:
- 35 g/¼ cup plain/all-purpose flour (gluten free if you wish)
- ½ teaspoon chilli/chili powder
- 1 egg, beaten
- 50 g/heaped ½ cup dried breadcrumbs (gluten-free if you wish; see page 9)
- 1 avocado, skin and stone removed, and each half sliced lengthways
- salt and freshly ground black pepper

Directions:
1. Preheat the air-fryer to 200°C/400°F.
2. In a bowl combine the flour and chilli/chili powder, then season with salt and pepper. Place the beaten egg in a second bowl and the breadcrumbs in a third bowl.
3. Dip each avocado slice in the seasoned flour (shaking off any excess), then the egg and finally the breadcrumbs.
4. Add the breaded avocado slices to the preheated air-fryer and air-fry for 6 minutes, turning after 4 minutes. Serve immediately.

Mexican Breakfast Burritos

Servings: 6
Cooking Time:xx

Ingredients:
- 6 scrambled eggs
- 6 medium tortillas
- Half a minced red pepper
- 8 sausages, cut into cubes and browned
- 4 pieces of bacon, pre-cooked and cut into pieces
- 65g grated cheese of your choice
- A small amount of olive oil for cooking

Directions:
1. Into a regular mixing bowl, combine the eggs, bell pepper, bacon pieces, the cheese, and the browned sausage, giving everything a good stir
2. Take your first tortilla and place half a cup of the mixture into the middle, folding up the top and bottom and rolling closed
3. Repeat until all your tortillas have been used
4. Arrange the burritos into the bottom of your fryer and spray with a little oil
5. Cook the burritos at 170°C for 5 minutes

Bocconcini Balls

Servings: 2
Cooking Time:xx

Ingredients:
- 70 g/½ cup plus ½ tablespoon plain/all-purpose flour (gluten-free if you wish)
- 1 egg, beaten
- 70 g/1 cup dried breadcrumbs (gluten-free if you wish; see page 9)
- 10 bocconcini

Directions:
1. Preheat the air-fryer to 200°C/400°F.
2. Place the flour, egg and breadcrumbs on 3 separate plates. Dip each bocconcini ball first in the flour to coat, then the egg, shaking off any excess before rolling in the breadcrumbs.
3. Add the breaded bocconcini to the preheated air-fryer and air-fry for 5 minutes (no need to turn them during cooking). Serve immediately.

Your Favourite Breakfast Bacon

Servings: 2
Cooking Time:xx

Ingredients:
- 4-5 rashers of lean bacon, fat cut off
- Salt and pepper for seasoning

Directions:
1. Line your air fryer basket with parchment paper
2. Place the bacon in the basket
3. Set the fryer to 200°C
4. Cook for 10 minutes for crispy. If you want it very crispy, cook for another 2 minutes

Easy Cheese & Bacon Toasties

Servings: 2
Cooking Time:xx

Ingredients:
- 4 slices of sandwich bread
- 2 slices of cheddar cheese
- 5 slices of pre-cooked bacon
- 1 tbsp melted butter
- 2 slices of mozzarella cheese

Directions:
1. Take the bread and spread the butter onto one side of each slice
2. Place one slice of bread into the fryer basket, buttered side facing downwards
3. Place the cheddar on top, followed by the bacon, mozzarella and the other slice of bread on top, buttered side upwards
4. Set your fryer to 170°C
5. Cook for 4 minutes and then turn over and cook for another 3 minutes
6. Serve whilst still hot

Sauces & Snack And Appetiser Recipes

Popcorn Tofu

Servings: 4
Cooking Time:xx

Ingredients:
- 400g firm tofu
- 100g chickpea flour
- 100g oatmeal
- 2 tbsp yeast
- 150ml milk
- 400g breadcrumbs
- 1 tsp garlic powder
- 1 tsp onion powder
- 1 tbsp dijon mustard
- ½ tsp salt
- ½ tsp pepper
- 2 tbsp vegetable bouillon

Directions:
1. Rip the tofu into pieces. Place the breadcrumbs into a bowl, in another bowl mix the remaining ingredients
2. Dip the tofu into the batter mix and then dip into the breadcrumbs
3. Heat the air fryer to 175ºC
4. Place the tofu in the air fryer and cook for 12 minutes shaking halfway through

Snack Style Falafel

Servings: 15
Cooking Time:xx

Ingredients:
- 150g dry garbanzo beans
- 300g coriander
- 75g flat leaf parsley
- 1 red onion, quartered
- 1 clove garlic
- 2 tbsp chickpea flour
- Cooking spray
- 1 tbsp cumin
- 1 tbsp coriander
- 1 tbsp sriracha
- ½ tsp baking powder
- Salt and pepper to taste
- ¼ tsp baking soda

Directions:
1. Add all ingredients apart from the baking soda and baking powder to a food processor and blend well
2. Cover and rest for 1 hour
3. Heat air fryer to 190ºC
4. Add baking powder and baking soda to mix and combine
5. Form mix into 15 equal balls
6. Spray air fryer with cooking spray
7. Add to air fryer and cook for 8-10 minutes

Mac & Cheese Bites

Servings: 14
Cooking Time:xx

Ingredients:
- 200g mac and cheese
- 2 eggs
- 200g panko breadcrumbs
- Cooking spray

Directions:
1. Place drops of mac and cheese on parchment paper and freeze for 1 hour
2. Beat the eggs in a bowl, add the breadcrumbs to another bowl
3. Dip the mac and cheese balls in the egg then into the breadcrumbs
4. Heat the air fryer to 190ºC
5. Place in the air fryer, spray with cooking spray and cook for 15 minutes

Garlic Pizza Toast

Servings: 8
Cooking Time:xx

Ingredients:
- 1 pack garlic Texas toast, or 8 slices of bread topped with garlic butter
- 100g pizza sauce
- 50g pepperoni
- 100g grated cheese

Directions:
1. Top each piece of toast with pizza sauce
2. Add cheese and pepperoni
3. Heat air fryer to 190ºC
4. Place in the air fryer and cook for 5 minutes

Mini Calzones

Servings: 16
Cooking Time:xx

Ingredients:
- Flour for rolling out the dough
- 1 round pizza dough
- 100g pizza sauce

Directions:
1. Roll out the dough to ¼ inch thick
2. Cut out 8-10 dough rounds using a cutter
3. Re-roll the dough and cut out another 6 rounds
4. Top each round with pizza sauce, cheese and pepperoni
5. Fold dough over and pinch the edges to seal
6. Heat the air fryer to 190ºC
7. Place the calzone in the air fryer and cook for about 8 minutes until golden brown

Thai Bites

Servings: 4
Cooking Time:xx

Ingredients:
- 400g pork mince
- 1 onion
- 1 tsp garlic paste
- 1 tbsp soy
- 1 tbsp Worcester sauce
- Salt and pepper
- 2 tsp Thai curry paste
- ½ lime juice and zest
- 1 tsp mixed spice
- 1 tsp Chinese spice
- 1 tsp coriander

Directions:
1. Place all ingredients in a bowl and mix well
2. Shape into balls
3. Place in the air fryer and cook at 180ºC for 15 minutes

Pasta Chips

Servings: 2
Cooking Time:xx

Ingredients:
- 300g dry pasta bows
- 1 tbsp olive oil
- 1 tbsp nutritional yeast
- 1½ tsp Italian seasoning
- ½ tsp salt

Directions:
1. Cook the pasta for half the time stated on the packet
2. Drain and mix with the oil, yeast, seasoning and salt
3. Place in the air fryer and cook at 200ºC for 5 minutes shake and cook for a further 3 minutes until crunchy

Cheese Wontons

Servings: 8
Cooking Time:xx

Ingredients:

- 8 wonton wrappers
- 1 carton pimento cheese
- Small dish of water
- Cooking spray

Directions:

1. Place one tsp of cheese in the middle of each wonton wrapper
2. Brush the edges of each wonton wrapper with water
3. Fold over to create a triangle and seal
4. Heat the air fryer to 190°C
5. Spray the wontons with cooking spray
6. Place in the air fryer and cook for 3 minutes
7. Turnover and cook for a further 3 minutes

Onion Bahji

Servings: 8
Cooking Time:xx

Ingredients:

- 1 sliced red onion
- 1 sliced onion
- 1 tsp salt
- 1 minced jalapeño pepper
- 150g chickpea flour
- 4 tbsp water
- 1 clove garlic, minced
- 1 tsp coriander
- 1 tsp chilli powder
- 1 tsp turmeric
- ½ tsp cumin

Directions:

1. Place all ingredients in a bowl and mix well, leave to rest for 10 minutes
2. Preheat air fryer to 175°C
3. Spray air fryer with cooking spray.
4. Form mix into bahji shapes and add to air fryer
5. Cook for 6 minutes turn and cook for a further 6 minutes

Chicken & Bacon Parcels

Servings: 4
Cooking Time:xx

Ingredients:
- 2 chicken breasts, boneless and skinless
- 200ml BBQ sauce
- 7 slices of bacon, cut lengthwise into halves
- 2 tbsp brown sugar

Directions:
1. Preheat the air fryer to 220°C
2. Cut the chicken into strips, you should have 7 in total
3. Wrap two strips of the bacon around each piece of chicken
4. Brush the BBQ sauce over the top and sprinkle with the brown sugar
5. Place the chicken into the basket and cook for 5 minutes
6. Turn the chicken over and cook for another 5 minutes

Asian Devilled Eggs

Servings: 12
Cooking Time:xx

Ingredients:
- 6 large eggs
- 2 tbsp mayo
- 1 ½ tsp sriracha
- 1 ½ tsp sesame oil
- 1 tsp soy sauce
- 1 tsp dijon mustard
- 1 tsp finely grated ginger
- 1 tsp rice vinegar
- 1 chopped green onion
- Toasted sesame seeds

Directions:
1. Set air fryer to 125°C
2. Place eggs in the air fryer and cook for 15 minutes
3. Remove from the air fryer and place in a bowl of iced water for 10 minutes
4. Peel and cut in half
5. Scoop out the yolks and place in a food processor
6. Add the ingredients apart from the sesame seeds and green onion and combine until smooth
7. Place in a piping bag and pipe back into the egg whites
8. Garnish with seeds and green onion

Stuffed Mushrooms

Servings: 24
Cooking Time:xx

Ingredients:
- 24 mushrooms
- ½ pepper, sliced
- ½ diced onion
- 1 small carrot, diced
- 200g grated cheese
- 2 slices bacon, diced
- 100g sour cream

Directions:
1. Place the mushroom stems, pepper, onion, carrot and bacon in a pan and cook for about 5 minutes
2. Stir in cheese and sour cream, cook until well combined
3. Heat the air fryer to 175°C
4. Add stuffing to each of the mushrooms
5. Place in the air fryer and cook for 8 minutes

Waffle Fries

Servings: 4
Cooking Time:xx

Ingredients:
- 2 large potatoes, russet potatoes work best
- 1 tsp salt for seasoning
- Waffle cutter

Directions:
1. Peel the potatoes and slice using the waffle cutter. You can also use a mandolin cutter that has a blade
2. Transfer the potatoes to a bowl and season with the salt, coating evenly
3. Add to the air fryer and cook at 220°C for 15 minutes, shaking every so often

Tasty Pumpkin Seeds

Servings: 2
Cooking Time:xx

Ingredients:
- 1 ¾ cups pumpkin seeds
- 2 tsp avocado oil
- 1 tsp paprika
- 1 tsp salt

Directions:
1. Preheat air fryer to 180°C
2. Add all ingredients to a bowl and mix well
3. Place in the air fryer and cook for 35 minutes shaking frequently

Lumpia

Servings: 16
Cooking Time:xx

Ingredients:
- 400g Italian sausage
- 1 sliced onion
- 1 chopped carrot
- 50g chopped water chestnuts
- Cooking spray
- 2 cloves minced, garlic
- 2 tbsp soy sauce
- ½ tsp salt
- ¼ tsp ground ginger
- 16 spring roll wrappers

Directions:
1. Cook sausage in a pan for about 5 minutes. Add green onions, onions, water chestnuts and carrot cook for 7 minutes
2. Add garlic and cook for a further 2 minutes
3. Add the soy sauce, salt and ginger, stir to mix well
4. Add filling to each spring roll wrapper.
5. Roll over the bottom and tuck in the sides, continue to roll up the spring roll
6. Spray with cooking spray and place in the air fryer
7. Cook at 200ºC for 4 minutes turn and cook for a further 4 minutes

Tortellini Bites

Servings: 6
Cooking Time:xx

Ingredients:
- 200g cheese tortellini
- 150g flour
- 100g panko bread crumbs
- 50g grated parmesan
- 1 tsp dried oregano
- 2 eggs
- ½ tsp garlic powder
- ½ tsp chilli flakes
- Salt
- Pepper

Directions:
1. Cook the tortellini according to the packet instructions
2. Mix the panko, parmesan, oregano, garlic powder, chilli flakes salt and pepper in a bowl
3. Beat the eggs in another bowl and place the flour in a third bowl
4. Coat the tortellini in flour, then egg and then in the panko mix
5. Place in the air fryer and cook at 185ºC for 10 minutes until crispy
6. Serve with marinara sauce for dipping

Corn Nuts

Servings: 8
Cooking Time:xx

Ingredients:
- 1 giant white corn
- 3 tbsp vegetable oil
- 2 tsp salt

Directions:
1. Place the corn in a large bowl, cover with water and sit for 8 hours
2. Drain, pat dry and air dry for 20 minutes
3. Preheat the air fryer to 200ºC
4. Place in a bowl and coat with oil and salt
5. Cook in the air fryer for 10 minutes shake then cook for a further 10 minutes

Onion Pakoda

Servings: 2
Cooking Time:xx

Ingredients:
- 200g gram flour
- 2 onions, thinly sliced
- 1 tbsp crushed coriander seeds
- 1 tsp chilli powder
- ¾ tsp salt
- ¼ tsp turmeric
- ¼ tsp baking soda

Directions:
1. Mix all the ingredients together in a large bowl
2. Make bite sized pakodas
3. Heat the air fryer to 200ºC
4. Line the air fryer with foil
5. Place the pakoda in the air fryer and cook for 5 minutes
6. Turn over and cook for a further 5 minutes

Air-fried Pickles

Servings: 4
Cooking Time:xx

Ingredients:

- 1/2 cup mayonnaise
- 2 tsp sriracha sauce
- 1 jar dill pickle slices
- 1 egg
- 2 tbsp milk
- 50g flour
- 50g cornmeal
- ½ tsp seasoned salt
- ¼ tsp paprika
- ¼ tsp garlic powder
- ⅛ tsp pepper
- Cooking spray

Directions:

1. Mix the mayo and sriracha together in a bowl and set aside
2. Heat the air fryer to 200ºC
3. Drain the pickles and pat dry
4. Mix egg and milk together, in another bowl mix all the remaining ingredients
5. Dip the pickles in the egg mix then in the flour mix
6. Spray the air fryer with cooking spray
7. Cook for about 4 minutes until crispy

Italian Rice Balls

Servings: 2
Cooking Time:xx

Ingredients:

- 400g cooked rice
- 25g breadcrumbs, plus an extra 200g for breading
- 2 tbsp flour, plus an extra 2 tbsp for breading
- 1 tbsp cornstarch, plus an extra 3 tbsp for breading
- 1 chopped bell pepper
- 1 chopped onion
- 2 tbsp olive oil
- 1 tsp red chilli flakes
- 5 chopped mozzarella cheese sticks
- A little water for the breading
- Salt and pepper for seasoning

Directions:

1. Place the cooked rice into a bowl and mash with a fork. Place to one side
2. Take a saucepan and add the oil, salting the onion and peppers until they're both soft
3. Add the chilli flakes and a little salt and combine
4. Add the mixture to the mashed rice and combine
5. Add the 2 tbsp flour and 1 tbsp cornstarch, along with the 25g breadcrumbs and combine well
6. Use your hands to create balls with the mixture
7. Stuff a piece of the mozzarella inside the balls and form around it
8. Take a bowl and add the rest of the flour, corn starch and a little seasoning, with a small amount of water to create a thick batter
9. Take another bowl and add the rest of the breadcrumbs
10. Dip each rice ball into the batter and then the breadcrumbs
11. Preheat the air fryer to 220ºC
12. Cook for 6 minutes, before shaking and cooking for another 6 minutes

Poultry Recipes

Chicken Milanese

Servings: 4
Cooking Time:xx

Ingredients:
- 130 g/1¾ cups dried breadcrumbs (gluten-free if you wish, see page 9)
- 50 g/⅔ cup grated Parmesan
- 1 teaspoon dried basil
- ½ teaspoon dried thyme
- ¼ teaspoon freshly ground black pepper
- 1 egg, beaten
- 4 tablespoons plain/all-purpose flour (gluten-free if you wish)
- 4 boneless chicken breasts

Directions:
1. Combine the breadcrumbs, cheese, herbs and pepper in a bowl. In a second bowl beat the egg, and in the third bowl have the plain/all-purpose flour. Dip each chicken breast first into the flour, then the egg, then the seasoned breadcrumbs.
2. Preheat the air-fryer to 180°C/350°F.
3. Add the breaded chicken breasts to the preheated air-fryer and air-fry for 12 minutes. Check the internal temperature of the chicken has reached at least 74°C/165°F using a meat thermometer – if not, cook for another few minutes.

Air Fryer Chicken Thigh Schnitzel

Servings: 4
Cooking Time:xx

Ingredients:
- 300g boneless chicken thighs
- 160g seasoned breadcrumbs
- 1 tsp salt
- ½ tsp ground black pepper
- 30g flour
- 1 egg
- Cooking spray

Directions:
1. Lay the chicken on a sheet of parchment paper and add another on top
2. Use a mallet or a rolling pin to flatten it down
3. Take a bowl and add the breadcrumbs with the salt and pepper
4. Place the flour into another bowl
5. Dip the chicken into the flour, then the egg, and then the breadcrumbs
6. Preheat air fryer to 190°C
7. Place the chicken into the air fryer and spray with cooking oil
8. Cook for 6 minutes

Thai Turkey Burgers

Servings: 4
Cooking Time:xx

Ingredients:

- 1 courgette/zucchini, about 200 g/7 oz.
- 400 g/14 oz. minced/ground turkey breast
- 35 g/½ cup fresh breadcrumbs (gluten-free if you wish)
- 1 teaspoon Thai 7 spice seasoning
- 1 teaspoon salt
- 1 teaspoon olive oil

Directions:

1. Coarsely grate the courgette/zucchini, then place in a piece of muslin/cheesecloth and squeeze out the water. Combine the grated courgette with all other ingredients except the olive oil, mixing together well. Divide the mixture into 4 equal portions and mould into burgers. Brush with oil.
2. Preheat the air-fryer to 190°C/375°C.
3. Add the turkey burgers to the preheated air-fryer and air-fry for 15 minutes, turning once halfway through cooking. Check the internal temperature of the burgers has reached at least 74°C/165°F using a meat thermometer – if not, cook for another few minutes and then serve.

Buffalo Wings

Servings: 4
Cooking Time:xx

Ingredients:

- 500g chicken wings
- 1 tbsp olive oil
- 5 tbsp cayenne pepper sauce
- 75g butter
- 2 tbsp vinegar
- 1 tsp garlic powder
- ¼ tsp cayenne pepper

Directions:

1. Preheat the air fryer to 182C
2. Take a large mixing bowl and add the chicken wings
3. Drizzle oil over the wings, coating evenly
4. Cook for 25 minutes and then flip the wings and cook for 5 more minutes
5. In a saucepan over a medium heat, mix the hot pepper sauce, butter, vinegar, garlic powder and cayenne pepper, combining well
6. Pour the sauce over the wings and flip to coat, before serving

Olive Stained Turkey Breast

Servings: 14
Cooking Time:xx

Ingredients:
- The brine from a can of olives
- 150ml buttermilk
- 300g boneless and skinless turkey breasts
- 1 sprig fresh rosemary
- 2 sprigs fresh thyme

Directions:
1. Take a mixing bowl and combine the olive brine and buttermilk
2. Pour the mixture over the turkey breast
3. Add the rosemary and thyme sprigs
4. Place into the refrigerator for 8 hours
5. Remove from the fridge and let the turkey reach room temperature
6. Preheat the air fryer to 175C
7. Cook for 15 minutes, ensuring the turkey is cooked through before serving

Healthy Bang Bang Chicken

Servings: 4
Cooking Time:xx

Ingredients:
- 500g chicken breasts, cut into pieces of around 1" in size
- 1 beaten egg
- 50ml milk
- 1 tbsp hot pepper sauce
- 80g flour
- 70g tapioca starch
- 1 ½ tsp seasoned starch
- 1 tsp garlic granules
- ½ tsp cumin
- 6 tbsp plain Greek yogurt
- 3 tbsp sweet chilli sauce
- 1 tsp hot sauce

Directions:
1. Preheat the air fryer to 190°C
2. Take a mixing bowl and combine the egg, milk and hot sauce
3. Take another bowl and combine the flour, tapioca starch, salt, garlic and cumin
4. Dip the chicken pieces into the sauce bowl and then into the flour bowl
5. Place the chicken into the air fryer
6. Whilst cooking, mix together the Greek yogurt, sweet chilli sauce and hot sauce and serve with the chicken

Chicken Parmesan With Marinara Sauce

Servings: 4
Cooking Time:xx

Ingredients:

- 400g chicken breasts, sliced in half
- 250g panko breadcrumbs
- 140g grated parmesan cheese
- 140g grated mozzarella cheese
- 3 egg whites
- 200g marinara sauce
- 2 tsp Italian seasoning
- Salt and pepper to taste
- Cooking spray

Directions:

1. Preheat the air fryer to 200°C
2. Lay the chicken slices on the work surface and pound with a mallet or a rolling pin to flatten
3. Take a mixing bowl and add the panko breadcrumbs, cheese and the seasoning, combining well
4. Add the egg whites into a separate bowl
5. Dip the chicken into the egg whites and then the breadcrumbs
6. Cook for 7 minutes in the air fryer

Chicken Tikka Masala

Servings: 4
Cooking Time:xx

Ingredients:

- 100g tikka masala curry pasta
- 200g low fat yogurt
- 600g skinless chicken breasts
- 1 tbsp vegetable oil
- 1 onion, chopped
- 400g can of the whole, peeled tomatoes
- 20ml water
- 1 tbsp sugar
- 2 tbsp lemon juice
- 1 small bunch of chopped coriander leaves

Directions:

1. Take a bowl and combine the tikka masala curry paste with half the yogurt
2. Cut the chicken into strips
3. Preheat the air fryer to 200°C
4. Add the yogurt mixture and coat the chicken until fully covered
5. Place into the refrigerator for 2 hours
6. Place the oil and onion in the air fryer and cook for 10 minutes
7. Add the marinated chicken, tomatoes, water and the rest of the yogurt and combine
8. Add the sugar and lemon juice and combine again
9. Cook for 15 minutes

Charred Chicken Breasts

Servings: 2
Cooking Time:xx

Ingredients:

- 2 tsp paprika
- 1 tsp ground thyme
- 1 tsp cumin
- ½ tsp cayenne pepper
- ½ tsp onion powder
- ½ tsp black pepper
- ¼ tsp salt
- 2 tsp vegetable oil
- 2 skinless boneless chicken breasts, cut into halves

Directions:

1. Take a bowl and add the paprika, thyme, cumin, cayenne pepper, onion powder, black pepper and salt
2. Coat each chicken breast with oil and dredge chicken in the spice mixture
3. Preheat air fryer to 175C
4. Cook for 10 minutes and flip
5. Cook for 10 more minutes

Pizza Chicken Nuggets

Servings: 2
Cooking Time:xx

Ingredients:

- 60 g/¾ cup dried breadcrumbs (see page 9)
- 20 g/¼ cup grated Parmesan
- ½ teaspoon dried oregano
- ¼ teaspoon freshly ground black pepper
- 150 g/⅔ cup Mediterranean sauce (see page 102) or 150 g/5½ oz. jarred tomato pasta sauce (keep any leftover sauce for serving)
- 400 g/14 oz. chicken fillets

Directions:

1. Preheat the air-fryer to 180°C/350°F.
2. Combine the breadcrumbs, Parmesan, oregano and pepper in a bowl. Have the Mediterranean or pasta sauce in a separate bowl.
3. Dip each chicken fillet in the tomato sauce first, then roll in the breadcrumb mix until coated fully.
4. Add the breaded fillets to the preheated air-fryer and air-fry for 10 minutes. Check the internal temperature of the chicken has reached at least 74°C/165°F using a meat thermometer – if not, cook for another few minutes.
5. Serve with some additional sauce that has been warmed through.

Chicken Fried Rice

Servings: 4
Cooking Time:xx

Ingredients:

- 400g cooked white rice
- 400g cooked chicken, diced
- 200g frozen peas and carrots
- 6 tbsp soy sauce
- 1 tbsp vegetable oil
- 1 diced onion

Directions:

1. Take a large bowl and add the rice, vegetable oil and soy sauce and combine well
2. Add the frozen peas, carrots, diced onion and the chicken and mix together well
3. Pour the mixture into a nonstick pan
4. Place the pan into the air fryer
5. Cook at 182C for 20 minutes

Nashville Chicken

Servings: 4
Cooking Time:xx

Ingredients:

- 400g boneless chicken breast tenders
- 2 tsp salt
- 2 tsp coarsely ground black pepper
- 2 tbsp hot sauce
- 2 tbsp pickle juice
- 500g all purpose flour
- 3 large eggs
- 300ml buttermilk
- 2 tbsp olive oil
- 6 tbsp cayenne pepper
- 3 tbsp dark brown sugar
- 1 tsp chilli powder
- 1 tsp garlic powder
- 1 tsp paprika
- Salt and pepper to taste

Directions:

1. Take a large mixing bowl and add the chicken, hot sauce, pickle juice, salt and pepper and combine
2. Place in the refrigerator for 3 hours
3. Transfer the flour to a bowl
4. Take another bowl and add the eggs, buttermilk and 1 tbsp of the hot sauce, combining well
5. Press each piece of chicken into the flour and coat well
6. Place the chicken into the buttermilk mixture and then back into the flour
7. Allow to sit or 10 minutes
8. Preheat the air fryer to 193C
9. Whisk together the spices, brown sugar and olive oil to make the sauce and pour over the chicken tenders
10. Serve whilst still warm

Chicken And Cheese Chimichangas

Servings: 6
Cooking Time:xx

Ingredients:

- 100g shredded chicken (cooked)
- 150g nacho cheese
- 1 chopped jalapeño pepper
- 6 flour tortillas
- 5 tbsp salsa
- 60g refried beans
- 1 tsp cumin
- 0.5 tsp chill powder
- Salt and pepper to taste

Directions:

1. Take a large mixing bowl and add all of the ingredients, combining well
2. Add ⅓ of the filling to each tortilla and roll into a burrito shape
3. Spray the air fryer with cooking spray and heat to 200ºC
4. Place the chimichangas in the air fryer and cook for 7 minutes

Pepper & Lemon Chicken Wings

Servings: 2
Cooking Time:xx

Ingredients:

- 1kg chicken wings
- 1/4 tsp cayenne pepper
- 2 tsp lemon pepper seasoning
- 3 tbsp butter
- 1 tsp honey
- An extra 1 tsp lemon pepper seasoning for the sauce

Directions:

1. Preheat the air fryer to 260ºC
2. Place the lemon pepper seasoning and cayenne in a bowl and combine
3. Coat the chicken in the seasoning
4. Place the chicken in the air fryer and cook for 20 minutes, turning over halfway
5. Turn the temperature up to 300ºC and cook for another 6 minutes
6. Meanwhile, melt the butter and combine with the honey and the rest of the seasoning
7. Remove the wings from the air fryer and pour the sauce over the top

Turkey Cutlets In Mushroom Sauce

Servings: 2
Cooking Time:xx

Ingredients:
- 2 turkey cutlets
- 1 tbsp butter
- 1 can of cream of mushroom sauce
- 160ml milk
- Salt and pepper for seasoning

Directions:
1. Preheat the air fryer to 220°C
2. Brush the turkey cults with the butter and seasoning
3. Place in the air fryer and cook for 11 minutes
4. Add the mushroom soup and milk to a pan and cook over the stone for around 10 minutes, stirring every so often
5. Top the turkey cutlets with the sauce

Chicken Kiev

Servings: 4
Cooking Time:xx

Ingredients:
- 4 boneless chicken breasts
- 4 tablespoons plain/all-purpose flour (gluten-free if you wish)
- 1 egg, beaten
- 130 g/2 cups dried breadcrumbs (gluten-free if you wish, see page 9)
- GARLIC BUTTER
- 60 g/4 tablespoons salted butter, softened
- 1 large garlic clove, finely chopped

Directions:

1. Mash together the butter and garlic. Form into a sausage shape, then slice into 4 equal discs. Place in the freezer until frozen.
2. Make a deep horizontal slit across each chicken breast, taking care not to cut through to the other side. Stuff the cavity with a disc of frozen garlic butter. Place the flour in a shallow bowl, the egg in another and the breadcrumbs in a third. Coat each chicken breast first in flour, then egg, then breadcrumbs.
3. Preheat the air-fryer to 180°C/350°F.
4. Add the chicken Kievs to the preheated air-fryer and air-fry for 12 minutes until cooked through. This is hard to gauge as the butter inside the breast is not an indicator of doneness, so test the meat in the centre with a meat thermometer – it should be at least 75°C/167°F; if not, cook for another few minutes.

Quick Chicken Nuggets

Servings: 4
Cooking Time:xx

Ingredients:

- 500g chicken tenders
- 25g ranch salad dressing mixture
- 2 tbsp plain flour
- 100g breadcrumbs
- 1 egg, beaten
- Olive oil spray

Directions:

1. Take a large mixing bowl and arrange the chicken inside
2. Sprinkle the seasoning over the top and ensure the chicken is evenly coated
3. Place the chicken to one side for around 10 minutes
4. Add the flour into a resealable bag
5. Crack the egg into a small mixing bowl and whisk
6. Pour the breadcrumbs onto a medium sized plate
7. Transfer the chicken into the resealable bag and coat with the flour, giving it a good shake
8. Remove the chicken and dip into the egg, and then rolling it into the breadcrumbs, coating evenly
9. Repeat with all pieces of the chicken
10. Heat your air fryer to 200°C
11. Arrange the chicken inside the fryer and add a little olive oil spray to avoid sticking
12. Cook for 4 minutes, before turning over and cooking for another 4 minutes
13. Remove and serve whilst hot

Honey Cajun Chicken Thighs

Servings: 6
Cooking Time:xx

Ingredients:

- 100ml buttermilk
- 1 tsp hot sauce
- 400g skinless, boneless chicken thighs
- 150g all purpose flour
- 60g tapioca flour
- 2.5 tsp cajun seasoning
- ½ tsp garlic salt
- ½ tsp honey powder
- ¼ tsp ground paprika
- ⅛ tsp cayenne pepper
- 4 tsp honey

Directions:

1. Take a large bowl and combine the buttermilk and hot sauce
2. Transfer to a plastic bag and add the chicken thighs
3. Allow to marinate for 30 minutes
4. Take another bowl and add the flour, tapioca flour, cajun seasoning, garlic, salt, honey powder, paprika, and cayenne pepper, combining well
5. Dredge the chicken through the mixture
6. Preheat the air fryer to 175C
7. Cook for 15 minutes before flipping the thighs over and cooking for another 10 minutes
8. Drizzle 1 tsp of honey over each thigh

Chicken & Potatoes

Servings: 4
Cooking Time:xx

Ingredients:

- 2 tbsp olive oil
- 2 potatoes, cut into 2" pieces
- 2 chicken breasts, cut into pieces of around 1" size
- 4 crushed garlic cloves
- 2 tsp smoked paprika
- 1 tsp thyme
- 1/2 tsp red chilli flakes
- Salt and pepper to taste

Directions:

1. Preheat your air fryer to 260ºC
2. Take a large bowl and combine the potatoes with half of the garlic, half the paprika, half the chilli flakes, salt, pepper and half the oil
3. Place into the air fryer and cook for 5 minutes, before turning over and cooking for another 5 minutes
4. Take a bowl and add the chicken with the rest of the seasonings and oil, until totally coated
5. Add the chicken to the potatoes mixture, moving the potatoes to the side
6. Cook for 10 minutes, turning the chicken halfway through

Orange Chicken

Servings: 2
Cooking Time:xx

Ingredients:

- 600g chicken thighs, boneless and skinless
- 2 tbsp cornstarch
- 60ml orange juice
- 1 tbsp soy sauce
- 2 tbsp brown sugar
- 1 tbsp rice wine vinegar
- 1/4 teaspoon ground ginger
- Pinch of red pepper flakes
- Zest of one orange
- 2 tsp water and 2 tsp cornstarch mixed together

Directions:

1. Preheat your air fryer to 250ºC
2. Take a bowl and combine the chicken with the cornstarch
3. Place in the air fryer and cook for 9 minutes
4. Take a bowl and combine the rest of the ingredients, except for the water and cornstarch mixture
5. Place in a saucepan and bring to the boil and then turn down to a simmer for 5 minutes
6. Add the water and cornstarch mixture to the pan and combine well
7. Remove the chicken from the fryer and pour the sauce over the top

Beef & Lamb And Pork Recipes

Old Fashioned Steak

Servings: 4
Cooking Time:xx

Ingredients:
- 4 medium steaks
- 100g flour
- ½ tsp garlic powder
- Salt and pepper
- 1 egg
- 4 slices bacon
- 350ml milk

Directions:
1. Beat the egg
2. Mix the flour with garlic powder, salt and pepper
3. Dip the steak into the egg then cover in the flour mix
4. Place in the air fryer and cook at 170°C for 7 minutes, turnover and cook for another 10 minutes until golden brown
5. Whilst the steak is cooking, place the bacon in a frying pan, stir in the flour. Add milk to the bacon and stir until there are no lumps in the flour
6. Season with salt and pepper Cook for 2 minutes until thickened season with salt and pepper

Roast Beef

Servings: 2
Cooking Time:xx

Ingredients:
- 400g beef fillet
- 1 tbsp olive oil
- 1 tsp salt
- 1 tsp rosemary

Directions:
1. Preheat the air fryer to 180°C
2. Mix salt, rosemary and oil on a plate
3. Coat the beef with the mix
4. Place the beef in the air fryer and cook for 45 minutes turning halfway

Tahini Beef Bites

Servings: 2
Cooking Time:xx

Ingredients:

- 500g sirloin steak, cut into cubes
- 2 tbsp Za'atar seasoning
- 1 tsp olive oil
- 25g Tahini
- 25g warm water
- 1 tbsp lemon juice
- 1 clove of garlic
- Salt to taste

Directions:

1. Preheat the air fryer to 250ºC
2. Take a bowl and combine the oil with the steak, salt, and Za'atar seasoning
3. Place in the air fryer and cook for 10 minutes, turning halfway through
4. Take a bowl and combine the water, garlic, lemon juice, salt, and tahini, or use a food processor if you have one
5. Pour the sauce over the bites and serve

Beef Satay

Servings: 2
Cooking Time:xx

Ingredients:

- 400g steak strips
- 2 tbsp oil
- 1 tbsp fish sauce
- 1 tsp sriracha sauce
- 200g sliced coriander (fresh)
- 1 tsp ground coriander
- 1 tbsp soy
- 1 tbsp minced ginger
- 1 tbsp minced garlic
- 1 tbsp sugar
- 25g roasted peanuts

Directions:

1. Add oil, dish sauce, soy, ginger, garlic, sugar sriracha, coriander and ¼ cup coriander to a bowl and mix. Add the steak and marinate for 30 minutes
2. Add the steak to the air fryer and cook at 200ºC for about 8 minutes
3. Place the steak on a plate and top with remaining coriander and chopped peanuts
4. Serve with peanut sauce

Pizza Dogs

Servings: 2
Cooking Time:xx

Ingredients:

- 2 pork hot dogs
- 4 pepperoni slices, halved
- 150g pizza sauce
- 2 hotdog buns
- 75g grated cheese
- 2 tsp sliced olives

Directions:

1. Preheat air fryer to 190ºC
2. Place 4 slits down each hotdog, place in the air fryer and cook for 3 minutes
3. Place a piece of pepperoni into each slit, add pizza sauce to hot dog buns
4. Place hotdogs in the buns and top with cheese and olives
5. Cook in the air fryer for about 2 minutes

Pork Taquitos

Servings: 5
Cooking Time:xx

Ingredients:

- 400g shredded pork
- 500g grated mozzarella
- 10 flour tortillas
- The juice of 1 lime
- Cooking spray

Directions:

1. Preheat air fryer to 190ºC
2. Sprinkle lime juice on the pork and mix
3. Microwave tortilla for about 10 seconds to soften
4. Add a little pork and cheese to a tortilla
5. Roll then tortilla up, and place in the air fryer
6. Cook for about 7 minutes until golden, turn halfway through cooking

Pulled Pork, Bacon, And Cheese Sliders

Servings:2
Cooking Time:30 Minutes

Ingredients:

- 2 x 50 g / 3.5 oz pork steaks
- 1 tsp salt
- 1 tsp black pepper
- 4 slices bacon strips, chopped into small pieces
- 1 tbsp soy sauce
- 1 tbsp BBQ sauce
- 100 g / 7 oz cheddar cheese, grated
- 2 bread buns

Directions:

1. Preheat the air fryer to 200 °C / 400 °F and line the bottom of the basket with parchment paper.
2. Place the pork steaks on a clean surface and season with salt and black pepper. Move the pork steak in the prepared air fryer basket and cook for 15 minutes.
3. Remove the steak from the air fryer and shred using two forks. Mix with the chopped bacon in a heatproof bowl and place the bowl in the air fryer. Cook for 10 minutes.
4. Remove the bowl from the air fryer and stir in the soy sauce and BBQ sauce. Return the bowl to the air fryer basket and continue cooking for a further 5 minutes.
5. Meanwhile, spread the cheese across one half of the bread buns. Top with the cooked pulled pork and an extra squirt of BBQ sauce.

Taco Lasagne Pie

Servings: 4
Cooking Time:xx

Ingredients:

- 450g ground beef
- 2 tbsp olive oil
- 1 chopped onion
- 1 minced garlic clove
- 1 tsp cumin
- 1 tsp oregano
- 1/2 tsp adobo
- 266g grated Cheddar cheese
- 4 flour tortillas
- 112g tomato sauce

Directions:

1. Soften the onions with the olive oil in a frying pan
2. Add the beef and garlic until the meat has browned
3. Add the tomato sauce, cumin, oregano, and adobo and combine
4. Allow to simmer for a few minutes
5. Place one tortilla on the bottom of your air fryer basket
6. Add a meat layer, followed by a layer of the cheese, and continue alternating this routine until you have no meat left
7. Add a tortilla on top and sprinkle with the rest of the cheese
8. Cook at 180°C for 8 minutes

Asparagus & Steak Parcels

Servings: 4
Cooking Time:xx

Ingredients:

- 500g flank steak, cut into 6 equal pieces
- 75ml Tamari sauce
- 2 crushed garlic cloves
- 250g trimmed asparagus
- 3 large bell peppers, thinly sliced
- 2 tbsp butter
- Salt and pepper to taste

Directions:

1. Season the steak to your liking
2. Place the meat in a zip top bag and add the Tamari and garlic, sealing the bag closed
3. Make sure the steaks are fully coated in the sauce and leave them in the fright at least 1 hour, but preferably overnight
4. Remove the steaks from the bag and throw the marinade away
5. Place the peppers and sliced asparagus in the centre of each steak piece
6. Roll the steak up and secure in place with a tooth pick
7. Preheat your air fryer to 250ºC
8. Transfer the meat parcels to the air fryer and cook for 5 minutes
9. Allow to rest before serving
10. Melt the butter in a saucepan, over a medium heat, adding the juices from the air fryer
11. Combine well and keep cooking until thickened
12. Pour the sauce over the steak parcels and season to your liking

Beef Bulgogi Burgers

Servings: 4
Cooking Time:xx

Ingredients:

- 500g minced beef
- 2 tbsp gochujang
- 1 tbsp soy
- 2 tsp minced garlic
- 2 tsp minced ginger
- 2 tsp sugar
- 1 tbsp olive oil
- 1 chopped onion

Directions:

1. Mix all the ingredients in a large bowl, allow to rest for at least 30 minutes in the fridge
2. Divide the meat into four and form into patties
3. Place in the air fryer and cook at 180ºC for about 10 minutes
4. Serve in burger buns, if desired

Meatballs In Tomato Sauce

Servings: 4
Cooking Time:xx

Ingredients:

- 1 small onion
- 300g minced pork
- 1 tbsp chopped parsley
- 1 tbsp thyme
- 1 egg
- 3 tbsp bread crumbs
- Salt and pepper to taste

Directions:

1. Place all ingredients into a bowl and mix well
2. Shape mixture into 12 meatballs
3. Heat the air fryer to 200°C
4. Place the meatballs into the air fryer and cook for about 7 minutes
5. Tip the meatballs into an oven dish add the tomato sauce and cook for about 5 minutes in the air fryer until warmed through

Sausage Burritos

Servings:4
Cooking Time:20 Minutes

Ingredients:

- 1 medium sweet potato
- 2 tbsp olive oil
- 1 tsp salt
- 1 tsp black pepper
- 8 sausages, uncooked
- 4 white flour tortillas
- 4 eggs, beaten
- 200 ml milk (any kind)
- 100 g / 3.5 oz cheddar cheese, grated

Directions:

1. Preheat the air fryer to 200 °C / 400 °F and line the air fryer mesh basket with parchment paper.
2. Peel the sweet potato and cut it into small chunks.
3. Place the sweet potato chunks in a bowl and toss in 1 tbsp olive oil. Sprinkle salt and pepper over the top.
4. Transfer the sweet potato chunks into the air fryer and cook for 8-10 minutes until hot. Remove from the air fryer and set aside to drain on paper towels.
5. Heat 1 tbsp olive oil in a medium frying pan and cook the sausages for 5-7 minutes until slightly browned. Remove the sausages and set them aside on paper towels to drain.
6. In a bowl, whisk together the beaten eggs and milk, and pour into the hot frying pan. Cook the eggs and use a fork to scramble them as they cook in the pan.
7. Once the eggs are cooked, mix them with the potatoes, sausages, and cheddar cheese in a bowl.
8. Spread the mixture evenly across the 4 white flour tortillas and roll them each up into tight burritos. Use a toothpick to keep them together if necessary.
9. Place the burritos into the hot air fryer and cook for 6-8 minutes, turning them over halfway through.
10. Enjoy the burritos for breakfast or lunch.

Pork Schnitzel

Servings: 2
Cooking Time:xx

Ingredients:

- 3 pork steaks, cut into cubes
- Salt and pepper
- 175g flour
- 2 eggs
- 175g breadcrumbs

Directions:

1. Sprinkle the pork with salt and pepper
2. Coat in the flour then dip in the egg
3. Coat the pork in breadcrumbs
4. Place in the air fryer and cook at 175ºC for 20 minutes turning halfway
5. Serve with red cabbage

Cheesy Meatballs

Servings: 2
Cooking Time:xx

Ingredients:

- 500g ground beef
- 1 can of chopped green chillis
- 1 egg white
- 1 tbsp water
- 2 tbsp taco seasoning
- 16 pieces of pepper jack cheese, cut into cubes
- 300g nacho cheese tortilla chips, crushed
- 6 tbsp taco sauce
- 3 tbsp honey

Directions:

1. Take a large bowl and combine the beef with the green collie sand taco seasoning
2. Use your hands to create meatballs - you should get around 15 balls in total
3. Place a cube of cheese in the middle of each meatball, forming the ball around it once more
4. Take a small bowl and beat the egg white
5. Take a large bowl and add the crushed chips
6. Dip every meatball into the egg white and then the crushed chips
7. Place the balls into the air fryer and cook at 260ºC for 14 minutes, turning halfway
8. Take a microwave-safe bowl and combine the honey and taco sauce
9. Place in the microwave for 30 seconds and serve the sauce warm with the meatballs

Tender Ham Steaks

Servings: 1
Cooking Time:xx

Ingredients:

- 1 ham steak
- 2 tbsp brown sugar
- 1 tsp honey
- 2 tbsp melted butter

Directions:

1. Preheat the air fryer to 220ºC
2. Combine the melted butter and brown sugar until smooth
3. Add the ham to the air fryer and brush both sides with the butter mixture
4. Cook for 12 minutes, turning halfway through and re-brushing the ham
5. Drizzle honey on top before serving

Pork Chops With Honey

Servings: 6
Cooking Time:xx

Ingredients:

- 2 ⅔ tbsp honey
- 100g ketchup
- 6 pork chops
- 2 cloves of garlic
- 2 slices mozzarella cheese

Directions:

1. Preheat air fryer to 200ºC
2. Mix all the ingredients together in a bowl
3. Add the pork chops, allow to marinate for at least 1 hour
4. Place in the air fryer and cook for about 12 minutes turning halfway

Parmesan Crusted Pork Chops

Servings: 6
Cooking Time:xx

Ingredients:
- 6 pork chops
- ½ tsp salt
- ¼ tsp pepper
- 1 tsp paprika
- 3 tbsp parmesan
- ½ tsp onion powder
- ¼ tsp chilli powder
- 2 eggs beaten
- 250g pork rind crumbs

Directions:
1. Preheat the air fryer to 200°C
2. Season the pork with the seasonings
3. Place the pork rind into a food processor and blend into crumbs
4. Mix the pork rind and seasonings in a bowl
5. Beat the eggs in a separate bowl
6. Dip the pork into the egg then into the crumb mix
7. Place pork in the air fryer and cook for about 15 minutes until crispy

Pork Chilli Cheese Dogs

Servings: 2
Cooking Time:xx

Ingredients:
- 1 can of pork chilli, or chilli you have left over
- 200g grated cheese
- 2 hot dog bread rolls
- 2 hot dogs

Directions:
1. Preheat the air fryer to 260°C
2. Cook the hot dogs for 4 minutes, turning halfway
3. Place the hotdogs inside the bread rolls and place back inside the air fryer
4. Top with half the cheese on top and then the chilli
5. Add the rest of the cheese
6. Cook for an extra 2 minutes

Hamburgers

Servings: 4
Cooking Time:xx

Ingredients:
- 500g minced beef
- 1 grated onion
- Salt and pepper to taste

Directions:
1. Preheat air fryer to 200ºC
2. Place the grated onion and the beef into a bowl and combine together well
3. Divide minced beef into 4 equal portions, form into patties
4. Season with salt and pepper
5. Place in the air fryer and cook for 10 minutes, turnover and cook for a further 3 minutes

Pork Chops With Raspberry And Balsamic

Servings: 4
Cooking Time:xx

Ingredients:
- 2 large eggs
- 30ml milk
- 250g panko bread crumbs
- 250g finely chopped pecans
- 1 tbsp orange juice
- 4 pork chops
- 30ml balsamic vinegar
- 2 tbsp brown sugar
- 2 tbsp raspberry jam

Directions:
1. Preheat air fryer to 200ºC
2. Mix the eggs and milk together in a bowl
3. In another bowl mix the breadcrumbs and pecans
4. Coat the pork chops in flour, egg and then coat in the breadcrumbs
5. Place in the air fryer and cook for 12 minutes until golden turning halfway
6. Put the remaining ingredients in a pan simmer for about 6 minutes, serve with the pork chops

Fish & Seafood Recipes

Parmesan-coated Fish Fingers

Servings: 2
Cooking Time:xx

Ingredients:
- 350 g/12 oz. cod loins
- 1 tablespoon grated Parmesan
- 40 g/½ cup dried breadcrumbs (gluten-free if you wish, see page 9)
- 1 egg, beaten
- 2 tablespoons plain/all-purpose flour (gluten free if you wish)

Directions:
1. Slice the cod into 6 equal fish fingers/sticks.
2. Mix the Parmesan together with the breadcrumbs. Lay out three bowls: one with flour, one with beaten egg and the other with the Parmesan breadcrumbs. Dip each fish finger/stick first into the flour, then the egg and then the breadcrumbs until fully coated.
3. Preheat the air-fryer to 180°C/350°F.
4. Add the fish to the preheated air-fryer and air-fry for 6 minutes. Check the internal temperature of the fish has reached at least 75°C/167°F using a meat thermometer – if not, cook for another few minutes. Serve immediately.

Lobster Tails

Servings: 2
Cooking Time:xx

Ingredients:
- 4 lobster tails
- 2 tbsp melted butter
- ½ tsp salt
- 1 tsp pepper

Directions:
1. Cut the lobster tails through the tail section and pull back the shell
2. Brush with the melted butter and sprinkle with salt and pepper
3. Heat the air fryer to 200°C and cook for 4 minutes
4. Brush with melted butter and cook for a further 2 minutes

Honey Sriracha Salmon

Servings: 2
Cooking Time:xx

Ingredients:
- 25g sriracha
- 25g honey
- 500g salmon fillets
- 1 tbsp soy sauce

Directions:
1. Mix the honey, soy sauce and sriracha, keep half the mix to one side for dipping
2. Place the salmon in the sauce skin side up and marinade for 30 minutes
3. Spray air fryer basket with cooking spray
4. Heat the air fryer to 200°C
5. Place salmon in the air fryer skin side down and cook for 12 minutes

Shrimp With Yum Yum Sauce

Servings: 4
Cooking Time:xx

Ingredients:
- 400g peeled jumbo shrimp
- 1 tbsp soy sauce
- 1 tbsp garlic paste
- 1 tbsp ginger paste
- 4 tbsp mayo
- 2 tbsp ketchup
- 1 tbsp sugar
- 1 tsp paprika
- 1 tsp garlic powder

Directions:
1. Mix soy sauce, garlic paste and ginger paste in a bowl. Add the shrimp, allow to marinate for 15 minutes
2. In another bowl mix ketchup, mayo, sugar, paprika and the garlic powder to make the yum yum sauce.
3. Set the air fryer to 200°C, place shrimp in the basket and cook for 8-10 minutes

Crispy Nacho Prawns

Servings: 6
Cooking Time:xx

Ingredients:
- 1 egg
- 18 large prawns
- 1 bag of nacho cheese flavoured corn chips, crushed

Directions:
1. Wash the prawns and pat dry
2. Place the chips into a bowl
3. In another bowl, whisk the egg
4. Dip the prawns into the egg and then the nachos
5. Preheat the air fryer to 180°C
6. Cook for 8 minutes

Store-cupboard Fishcakes

Servings: 3
Cooking Time:xx

Ingredients:

- 400 g/14 oz. cooked potato – either mashed potato or the insides of jacket potatoes (see page 124)
- 2 x 150–200-g/5½–7-oz. cans fish, such as tuna or salmon, drained
- 2 eggs
- ¾ teaspoon salt
- 1 teaspoon dried parsley
- ½ teaspoon freshly ground black pepper
- 1 tablespoon olive oil
- caper dressing (see page 79), to serve

Directions:

1. Mix the cooked potato, fish, eggs, salt, parsley and pepper together in a bowl, then divide into 6 equal portions and form into fishcakes. Drizzle the olive oil over both sides of each fishcake.
2. Preheat the air-fryer to 180°C/350°F.
3. Add the fishcakes to the preheated air-fryer and air-fry for 15 minutes, turning halfway through cooking. Serve with salad and tartare sauce or Caper Dressing.

Garlic Tilapia

Servings: 2
Cooking Time:xx

Ingredients:

- 2 tilapia fillets
- 2 tsp chopped fresh chives
- 2 tsp chopped fresh parsley
- 2 tsp olive oil
- 1 tsp minced garlic
- Salt and pepper for seasoning

Directions:

1. Preheat the air fryer to 220°C
2. Take a small bowl and combine the olive oil with the chives, garlic, parsley and a little salt and pepper
3. Brush the mixture over the fish fillets
4. Place the fish into the air fryer and cook for 10 minutes, until flaky

Traditional Fish And Chips

Servings: 4
Cooking Time:xx

Ingredients:
- 4 potatoes, peeled and cut into chips
- 2 fish fillets of your choice
- 1 beaten egg
- 3 slices of wholemeal bread, grated into breadcrumbs
- 25g tortilla crisps
- 1 lemon rind and juice
- 1 tbsp parsley
- Salt and pepper to taste

Directions:
1. Preheat your air fryer to 200ºC
2. Place the chips inside and cook until crispy
3. Cut the fish fillets into 4 slices and season with lemon juice
4. Place the breadcrumbs, lemon rind, parsley, tortillas and seasoning into a food processor and blitz to create a crumb consistency
5. Place the breadcrumbs on a large plate
6. Coat the fish in the egg and then the breadcrumb mixture
7. Cook for 15 minutes at 180ºC

Fish In Parchment Paper

Servings: 2
Cooking Time:xx

Ingredients:
- 250g cod fillets
- 1 chopped carrot
- 1 chopped fennel
- 1 tbsp oil
- 1 thinly sliced red pepper
- ½ tsp tarragon
- 1 tbsp lemon juice
- 1 tbsp salt
- ½ tsp ground pepper

Directions:
1. In a bowl, mix the tarragon and ½ tsp salt add the vegetables and mix well
2. Cut two large squares of parchment paper
3. Spray the cod with oil and cover both sides with salt and pepper
4. Place the cod in the parchment paper and add the vegetables
5. Fold over the paper to hold the fish and vegetables
6. Place in the air fryer and cook at 170ºC for 15 minutes

Crunchy Fish

Servings: 4
Cooking Time:xx

Ingredients:
- 200g dry breadcrumbs
- 4 tbsp olive oil
- 4 fillets of white fish
- 1 beaten egg
- 1 sliced lemon

Directions:
1. Heat the fryer to 180ºC
2. In a medium mixing bowl, combine the olive oil and the breadcrumbs
3. Take the fish and first dip it into the egg and then the breadcrumbs, making sure they are evenly coated well
4. Arrange the fish into the basket
5. Cook for 12 minutes
6. Remove and serve with lemon slices

Fish Taco Cauliflower Rice Bowls

Servings: 2
Cooking Time:xx

Ingredients:
- 400g fish of your choice, cut into strips
- 1 tsp chilli powder
- ½ tsp paprika
- 1 sliced avocado
- 25g pickled red onions
- 25g reduced fat sour cream
- ½ tsp cumin
- Salt and pepper to taste
- 300g cauliflower rice
- 1 tbsp lime juice
- 25g fresh coriander
- 1 tbsp sriracha

Directions:
1. Sprinkle both sides of the fish with chilli powder, cumin, paprika, salt and pepper
2. Heat the air fryer to 200ºC, cook the fish for about 12 minutes
3. cook the cauliflower rice according to instructions, mix in lime juice and coriander once cooked
4. Divide the cauliflower rice between two bowls, add the sliced avocado, fish and pickled red onions.
5. Mix the sour cream with the sriracha and drizzle over the top

Garlic Butter Salmon

Servings: 2
Cooking Time:xx

Ingredients:

- 2 salmon fillets, boneless with the skin left on
- 1 tsp minced garlic
- 2 tbsp melted butter
- 1 tsp chopped parsley
- Salt and pepper to taste

Directions:

1. Preheat the air fryer to 270 ºC
2. Take a bowl and combine the melted butter, parsley and garlic to create a sauce
3. Season the salmon to your liking
4. Brush the salmon with the garlic mixture, on both sides
5. Place the salmon into the fryer, with the skin side facing down
6. Cook for 10 minutes - the salmon is done when it flakes with ease

Cod Nuggets

Servings: 4
Cooking Time:xx

Ingredients:

- 400g cod fillets, cut into 8 chunks
- 35g flour
- 1 tbsp vegetable oil
- 200g cornflakes or cracker crumbs
- Egg wash - 1 tbsp egg and 1 tbsp water
- Salt and pepper to taste

Directions:

1. Crush the crackers or cornflakes to make crumbs, mix in the vegetable oil
2. Season the cod with salt and pepper and cover in flour, dip into the egg-wash then cover in crumbs
3. Set the air fryer to 180ºC
4. Place the cod nuggets in the air fryer basket and cook for 15 minutes, until golden brown.

Fish In Foil

Servings: 2
Cooking Time:xx

Ingredients:

- 1 tablespoon avocado oil or olive oil, plus extra for greasing
- 1 tablespoon soy sauce (or tamari)
- 1½ teaspoons freshly grated garlic
- 1½ teaspoons freshly grated ginger
- 1 small red chilli/chile, finely chopped
- 2 skinless, boneless white fish fillets (about 350 g/12 oz. total weight)

Directions:

1. Mix the oil, soy sauce, garlic, ginger and chilli/chile together. Brush a little oil onto two pieces of foil, then lay the fish in the centre of the foil. Spoon the topping mixture over the fish. Wrap the foil around the fish to make a parcel, with a gap above the fish but shallow enough to fit in your air-fryer basket.
2. Preheat the air-fryer to 180ºC/350ºF.
3. Add the foil parcels to the preheated air-fryer and air-fry for 7–10 minutes, depending on the thickness of your fillets. The fish should just flake when a fork is inserted. Serve immediately.

Copycat Fish Fingers

Servings: 2
Cooking Time:xx

Ingredients:

- 2 slices wholemeal bread, grated into breadcrumbs
- 50g plain flour
- 1 beaten egg
- 1 white fish fillet
- The juice of 1 small lemon
- 1 tsp parsley
- 1 tsp thyme
- 1 tsp mixed herbs
- Salt and pepper to taste

Directions:

1. Preheat the air fryer to 180ºC
2. Add salt pepper and parsley to the breadcrumbs and combine well
3. Place the egg in another bowl
4. Place the flour in a separate bowl
5. Place the fish into a food processor and add the lemon juice, salt, pepper thyme and mixed herbs
6. Blitz to create a crumb-like consistency
7. Roll your fish in the flour, then the egg and then the breadcrumbs
8. Cook at 180ºC for 8 minutes

Maine Seafood

Servings: 2
Cooking Time:xx

Ingredients:

- 500g flour
- 400g breadcrumbs
- 300g steamer clams
- 3 eggs
- 3 tbsp water

Directions:

1. Soak the clams for 3 hours, drain and rinse
2. Bring 1 inch of water to boil, add the clams and cover with a lid, steam for about 7 minutes until the clams open.
3. Remove the clams from the shell and set aside
4. Put the eggs in a bowl and mix with the water
5. Dip the clams in the flour, then the egg and then coat in breadcrumbs
6. Heat the air fryer to 180ºC and cook for about 7 minutes

Shrimp Wrapped With Bacon

Servings: 2
Cooking Time:xx

Ingredients:

- 16 shrimp
- 16 slices of bacon
- 2 tbsp ranch dressing to serve

Directions:

1. Preheat the air fryer to 200ºC
2. Wrap the shrimps in the bacon
3. Refrigerate for 30 minutes
4. Cook the shrimp for about 5 minutes turn them over and cook for a further 2 minutes
5. Serve with the ranch dressing on the side

Thai Salmon Patties

Servings: 7
Cooking Time:xx

Ingredients:

- 1 large can of salmon, drained and bones removed
- 30g panko breadcrumbs
- ¼ tsp salt
- 1 ½ tbsp Thai red curry paste
- 1 ½ tbsp brown sugar
- Zest of 1 lime
- 2 eggs
- Cooking spray

Directions:

1. Take a large bowl and combine all ingredients together until smooth
2. Use your hands to create patties that are around 1 inch in thickness
3. Preheat your air fryer to 180ºC
4. Coat the patties with cooking spray
5. Cook for 4 minutes each side

Air Fried Scallops

Servings: 2
Cooking Time:xx

Ingredients:
- 6 scallops
- 1 tbsp olive oil
- Salt and pepper to taste

Directions:
1. Brush the filets with olive oil
2. Sprinkle with salt and pepper
3. Place in the air fryer and cook at 200ºC for 2 mins
4. Turn the scallops over and cook for another 2 minutes

Oat & Parmesan Crusted Fish Fillets

Servings: 2
Cooking Time:xx

Ingredients:
- 20 g/⅓ cup fresh breadcrumbs
- 25 g/3 tablespoons oats
- 15 g/¼ cup grated Parmesan
- 1 egg
- 2 x 175-g/6-oz. white fish fillets, skin-on
- salt and freshly ground black pepper

Directions:

1. Preheat the air-fryer to 180ºC/350ºF.

2. Combine the breadcrumbs, oats and cheese in a bowl and stir in a pinch of salt and pepper. In another bowl beat the egg. Dip the fish fillets in the egg, then top with the oat mixture.

3. Add the fish fillets to the preheated air-fryer on an air-fryer liner or a piece of pierced parchment paper. Air-fry for 10 minutes. Check the fish is just flaking away when a fork is inserted, then serve immediately.

Vegetarian & Vegan Recipes

Veggie Lasagne

Servings: 1
Cooking Time:xx

Ingredients:
- 2 lasagne sheets
- Pinch of salt
- 100g pasta sauce
- 50g ricotta
- 60g chopped basil
- 40g chopped spinach
- 3 tbsp grated courgette

Directions:
1. Break the lasagne sheets in half, bring a pan of water to boil
2. Cook the lasagne sheets for about 8 minutes, drain and pat dry
3. Add 2 tbsp of pasta sauce to a mini loaf tin
4. Add a lasagne sheet, top with ricotta, basil and spinach, then add courgette
5. Place another lasagne sheet on top
6. Add a couple of tbsp pasta sauce, basil, spinach and courgette
7. Add the last lasagne sheet, top with pasta sauce and ricotta
8. Cover with foil and place in the air fryer
9. Cook at 180ºC for 10 mins, remove foil and cook for another 3 minutes

Courgette Meatballs

Servings: 4
Cooking Time:xx

Ingredients:
- 400g oats
- 40g feta, crumbled
- 1 beaten egg
- Salt and pepper
- 150g courgette
- 1 tsp lemon rind
- 6 basil leaves, thinly sliced
- 1 tsp dill
- 1 tsp oregano

Directions:
1. Preheat the air fryer to 200ºC
2. Grate the courgette into a bowl, squeeze any access water out
3. Add all the remaining ingredients apart from the oats and mix well
4. Blend the oats until they resemble breadcrumbs
5. Add the oats into the other mix and stir well
6. Form into balls and place in the air fryer cook for 10 minutes

Ratatouille

Servings: 4
Cooking Time:xx

Ingredients:

- ½ small aubergine, cubed
- 1 courgette, cubed
- 1 tomato, cubed
- 1 pepper, cut into cubes
- ½ onion, diced
- 1 fresh cayenne pepper, sliced
- 1 tsp vinegar
- 5 sprigs basil, chopped
- 2 sprigs oregano, chopped
- 1 clove garlic, crushed
- Salt and pepper
- 1 tbsp olive oil
- 1 tbsp white wine

Directions:

1. Preheat air fryer to 200ºC
2. Place all ingredients in a bowl and mix
3. Pour into a baking dish
4. Add dish to the air fryer and cook for 8 minutes, stir then cook for another 10 minutes

Two-step Pizza

Servings: 1
Cooking Time:xx

Ingredients:

- BASE
- 130 g/generous ½ cup Greek yogurt
- 125 g self-raising/self-rising flour, plus extra for dusting
- ¼ teaspoon salt
- PIZZA SAUCE
- 100 g/3½ oz. passata/strained tomatoes
- 1 teaspoon dried oregano
- ¼ teaspoon garlic salt
- TOPPINGS
- 75 g/2½ oz. mozzarella, torn
- fresh basil leaves, to garnish

Directions:

1. Mix together the base ingredients in a bowl. Once the mixture starts to look crumbly, use your hands to bring the dough together into a ball. Transfer to a piece of floured parchment paper and roll to about 5 mm/¼ in. thick. Transfer to a second piece of non-floured parchment paper.
2. Preheat the air-fryer to 200ºC/400ºF.
3. Meanwhile, mix the pizza sauce ingredients together in a small bowl and set aside.
4. Prick the pizza base all over with a fork and transfer (on the parchment paper) to the preheated air-fryer and air-fry for 5 minutes. Turn the pizza base over and top with the pizza sauce and the torn mozzarella. Cook for a further 3–4 minutes, until the cheese has melted. Serve immediately with the basil scattered over the top.

Stuffed Peppers

Servings: 6
Cooking Time:xx

Ingredients:

- 250g diced potatoes
- 100g peas
- 1 small onion, diced
- 1 carrot, diced
- 1 bread roll, diced
- 2 garlic cloves, minced
- 2 tsp mixed herbs
- 6 bell peppers
- 100g grated cheese

Directions:

1. Preheat air fryer to 180ºC
2. Combine all the ingredients together apart from the peppers
3. Stuff the peppers with the mix
4. Place in the air fryer and cook for about 20 minutes

Vegetarian "chicken" Tenders

Servings: 4
Cooking Time:xx

Ingredients:

- 250g flour
- 3 eggs
- 100g panko bread crumbs
- 1 tsp garlic powder
- 2 packs of vegetarian chicken breasts
- ¾ tsp paprika
- ½ tsp cayenne
- ½ tsp pepper
- ½ tsp chilli powder
- ½ tsp salt

Directions:

1. Pour flour onto a plate, beat eggs into a bowl. Combine all remaining dry ingredients in a bowl
2. Cut the chicken into strips
3. Dip the chicken in flour, then egg and then into the breadcrumb mix
4. Heat the air fryer to 260ºC
5. Cook for 6 minutes turn and then cook for another 6 minutes until golden brown

Air Fryer Cheese Sandwich

Servings:2
Cooking Time:10 Minutes

Ingredients:
- 4 slices white or wholemeal bread
- 2 tbsp butter
- 50 g / 3.5 oz cheddar cheese, grated

Directions:
1. Preheat the air fryer to 180 °C / 350 °F and line the bottom of the basket with parchment paper.
2. Lay the slices of bread out on a clean surface and butter one side of each. Evenly sprinkle the cheese on two of the slices and cover with the final two slices.
3. Transfer the sandwiches to the air fryer, close the lid, and cook for 5 minutes until the bread is crispy and golden, and the cheese is melted.

Air-fried Artichoke Hearts

Servings: 7
Cooking Time:xx

Ingredients:
- 14 artichoke hearts
- 200g flour
- ¼ tsp baking powder
- Salt
- 6 tbsp water
- 6 tbsp breadcrumbs
- ¼ tsp basil
- ¼ tsp oregano
- ¼ tsp garlic powder
- ¼ tsp paprika

Directions:
1. Mix the baking powder, salt, flour and water in a bowl
2. In another bowl combine the breadcrumbs and seasonings
3. Dip the artichoke in the batter then coat in breadcrumbs
4. Place in the air fryer and cook at 180°C for 8 minutes

Baked Feta, Tomato & Garlic Pasta

Servings: 2
Cooking Time:xx

Ingredients:
- 100 g/3½ oz. feta or plant-based feta, cubed
- 20 cherry tomatoes
- 2 garlic cloves, peeled and halved
- ¾ teaspoon oregano
- 1 teaspoon chilli/hot red pepper flakes
- ½ teaspoon garlic salt
- 2 tablespoons olive oil
- 100 g/3½ oz. cooked pasta plus about 1 tablespoon of cooking water
- freshly ground black pepper

Directions:
1. Preheat the air-fryer to 200°C/400°F.
2. Place the feta, tomatoes and garlic in a baking dish that fits inside your air-fryer. Top with the oregano, chilli/hot red pepper flakes, garlic salt and olive oil. Place the dish in the preheated air-fryer and air-fry for 10 minutes, then remove and stir in the pasta and cooking water. Serve sprinkled with black pepper.

Satay Tofu Skewers

Servings: 2
Cooking Time:xx

Ingredients:
- 300 g/10½ oz. firm tofu
- Lime-Almond Satay Sauce (see page 87), to serve
- MARINADE
- 200 ml/¾ cup coconut milk (including the thick part from the can)
- 1 plump garlic clove, finely chopped
- 2 teaspoons grated ginger
- 2 tablespoons soy sauce
- 1 heaped tablespoon smooth peanut butter
- 1 tablespoon maple syrup
- 1 tablespoon mild curry powder
- 1 tablespoon fish sauce or plant-based alternative

Directions:
1. Cut the tofu into 2 x 2-cm/¾ x ¾-in. cubes. Mix the marinade ingredients thoroughly, then toss in the tofu cubes. Once the tofu cubes are covered in the marinade, leave in the fridge to marinate for at least 4 hours.
2. Preheat the air-fryer to 180°C/350°F.
3. Thread the tofu cubes onto 4 skewers that fit inside your air-fryer. Place on an air-fryer liner or a piece of pierced parchment paper and add to the preheated air-fryer. Air-fry for 12 minutes, turning over once during cooking.
4. Serve the tofu skewers alongside a bowl of the Lime-Almond Satay Sauce.

Macaroni & Cheese Quiche

Servings: 4
Cooking Time:xx

Ingredients:
- 8 tbsp macaroni pasta
- 1 block of short crust pastry
- 2 tbsp Greek yogurt
- 2 eggs
- 150ml milk
- 1 tsp garlic puree
- 400g grated cheese

Directions:
1. Rub the inside of 4 ramekins with flour
2. Line the ramekins with the pastry
3. Mix the yogurt, garlic and macaroni. Add to the ramekins until ¾ full
4. Mix the egg and milk together and pour over the macaroni. Sprinkle with cheese
5. Heat the air fryer to 180ºC and cook for 20 minutes until golden brown.

Mini Quiche

Servings: 2
Cooking Time:xx

Ingredients:
- 100g raw cashews
- 3 tbsp milk
- ½ tsp hot sauce
- 1 tsp white miso paste
- 1 tsp mustard
- 300g tofu
- 100g bacon pieces
- 1 chopped red pepper
- 1 chopped onion
- 6 tbsp yeast
- ½ tsp onion powder
- ½ tsp paprika
- ½ tsp cumin
- ½ tsp chilli powder
- ½ tsp black pepper
- ⅛ tsp turmeric
- ½ tsp canola oil
- 50g curly kale

Directions:
1. Heat the oil in a pan, add the bacon pepper, onion and curly kale and cook for about 3 minutes
2. Place all the other ingredients into a blender and blend until smooth
3. Add to a bowl with the bacon, pepper, onion and curly kale and mix well
4. Fill silicone muffin cups with the mix
5. Place in the air fryer and cook at 165ºC for 15 minutes

Roasted Vegetable Pasta

Servings:4
Cooking Time:15 Minutes

Ingredients:
- 400 g / 14 oz penne pasta
- 1 courgette, sliced
- 1 red pepper, deseeded and sliced
- 100 g / 3.5 oz mushroom, sliced
- 2 tbsp olive oil
- 1 tsp Italian seasoning
- 200 g cherry tomatoes, halved
- 2 tbsp fresh basil, chopped
- ½ tsp black pepper

Directions:
1. Cook the pasta according to the packet instructions.
2. Preheat the air fryer to 190 °C / 370 °F and line the air fryer with parchment paper or grease it with olive oil.
3. In a bowl, place the courgette, pepper, and mushroom, and toss in 2 tbsp olive oil
4. Place the vegetables in the air fryer and cook for 15 minutes.
5. Once the vegetables have softened, mix with the penne pasta, chopped cherry tomatoes, and fresh basil.
6. Serve while hot with a sprinkle of black pepper in each dish.

Baked Aubergine Slices With Yogurt Dressing

Servings: 2
Cooking Time:xx

Ingredients:
- 1 aubergine/eggplant, sliced 1.5 cm/⅝ in. thick
- 3 tablespoons olive oil
- ½ teaspoon salt
- YOGURT DRESSING
- 1 small garlic clove
- 1 tablespoon tahini or nut butter
- 100 g/½ cup Greek yogurt
- 2 teaspoons freshly squeezed lemon juice
- 1 tablespoon runny honey
- a pinch of salt
- a pinch of ground cumin
- a pinch of sumac
- TO SERVE
- 30 g/1 oz. rocket/arugula
- 2 tablespoons freshly chopped mint
- 3 tablespoons pomegranate seeds

Directions:
1. Preheat the air-fryer to 180ºC/350ºF.
2. Drizzle the olive oil over each side of the aubergine/eggplant slices. Sprinkle with salt. Add the aubergines to the preheated air-fryer and air-fry for 10 minutes, turning halfway through cooking.
3. Meanwhile, make the dressing by combining all the ingredients in a mini food processor (alterantively, finely chop the garlic, add to a jar with the other ingredients and shake vigorously).
4. Serve the cooked aubergine slices on a bed of rocket/arugula, drizzled with the dressing and with the mint and pomegranate seeds scattered over the top.

Vegan Fried Ravioli

Servings: 4
Cooking Time:xx

Ingredients:

- 100g panko breadcrumbs
- 2 tsp yeast
- 1 tsp basil
- 1 tsp oregano
- 1 tsp garlic powder
- Pinch salt and pepper
- 50ml liquid from can of chickpeas
- 150g vegan ravioli
- Cooking spray
- 50g marinara for dipping

Directions:

1. Combine the breadcrumbs, yeast, basil, oregano, garlic powder and salt and pepper
2. Put the liquid from the chickpeas in a bowl
3. Dip the ravioli in the liquid then dip into the breadcrumb mix
4. Heat the air fryer to 190ºC
5. Place the ravioli in the air fryer and cook for about 6 minutes until crispy

Artichoke Crostini

Servings: 2
Cooking Time:xx

Ingredients:

- 100g cashews
- 1 tbsp olive oil
- 1 tbsp lemon juice
- 1 tsp balsamic vinegar
- 3 tbsp hummus
- 200g grilled artichoke hearts
- ½ tsp basil
- ½ tsp oregano
- ⅛ tsp onion powder
- 1 clove garlic minced
- Salt
- 1 baguette cut in ½ inch slices

Directions:

1. Combine cashews, olive oil, lemon juice, balsamic vinegar, basil oregano, onion powder, garlic and salt in a bowl. Set aside
2. Place the baguette slices in the air fryer and cook at 180ºC for 3-4 minutes
3. Sprinkle the baguette slices with cashew mix then add the artichoke hearts
4. Serve with hummus

Falafel Burgers

Servings: 2
Cooking Time:xx

Ingredients:

- 1 large can of chickpeas
- 1 onion
- 1 lemon
- 140g oats
- 28g grated cheese
- 28g feta cheese
- Salt and pepper to taste
- 3 tbsp Greek yogurt
- 4 tbsp soft cheese
- 1 tbsp garlic puree
- 1 tbsp coriander
- 1 tbsp oregano
- 1 tbsp parsley

Directions:

1. Place the chickpeas, onion, lemon rind, garlic and seasonings and blend until coarse
2. Add the mix to a bowl and stir in half the soft cheese, cheese and feta
3. Form in to burger shape and coat in the oats
4. Place in the air fryer and cook at 180ºC for 8 minutes
5. To make the sauce mix the remaining soft cheese, greek yogurt and lemon juice in a bowl

Artichoke Pasta

Servings: 2
Cooking Time:xx

Ingredients:

- 100g pasta
- 50g basil leaves
- 6 artichoke hearts
- 2 tbsp pumpkin seeds
- 2 tbsp lemon juice
- 1 clove garlic
- ½ tsp white miso paste
- 1 can chickpeas
- 1 tsp olive oil

Directions:

1. Place the chickpeas in the air fryer and cook at 200ºC for 12 minutes
2. Cook the pasta according to packet instructions
3. Add the remaining ingredients to a food processor and blend
4. Add the pasta to a bowl and spoon over the pesto mix
5. Serve and top with roasted chickpeas

Aubergine Parmigiana

Servings: 2 As A Main Or 4 As A Side
Cooking Time:xx

Ingredients:

- 2 small or 1 large aubergine/eggplant, sliced 5 mm/¼ in. thick
- 1 tablespoon olive oil
- ¾ teaspoon salt
- 200 g/7 oz. mozzarella, sliced
- ½ teaspoon freshly ground black pepper
- 20 g/¼ cup finely grated Parmesan
- green vegetables, to serve
- SAUCE
- 135 g/5 oz. passata/strained tomatoes
- 1 teaspoon dried oregano
- ¼ teaspoon garlic salt
- 1 tablespoon olive oil

Directions:

1. Preheat the air-fryer to 200ºC/400ºF.
2. Rub each of the aubergine/eggplant slices with olive oil and salt. Divide the slices into two batches. Place one batch of the aubergine slices in the preheated air-fryer and air-fry for 4 minutes on one side, then turn over and air-fry for 2 minutes on the other side. Lay these on the base of a gratin dish that fits into your air-fryer.
3. Air-fry the second batch of aubergine slices in the same way. Whilst they're cooking, mix together the sauce ingredients in a small bowl.
4. Spread the sauce over the aubergines in the gratin dish. Add a layer of the mozzarella slices, then season with pepper. Add a second layer of aubergine slices, then top with Parmesan.
5. Place the gratin dish in the air-fryer and air-fry for 6 minutes, until the mozzarella is melted and the top of the dish is golden brown. Serve immediately with green vegetables on the side.

Crispy Potato Peels

Servings: 1
Cooking Time:xx

Ingredients:

- Peels from 4 potatoes
- Cooking spray
- Salt to season

Directions:

1. Heat the air fryer to 200ºC
2. Place the peels in the air fryer spray with oil and sprinkle with salt
3. Cook for about 6-8 minutes until crispy

Side Dishes Recipes

Crispy Broccoli

Servings: 2
Cooking Time:xx

Ingredients:
- 170 g/6 oz. broccoli florets
- 2 tablespoons olive oil
- ⅛ teaspoon garlic salt
- ⅛ teaspoon freshly ground black pepper
- 2 tablespoons freshly grated Parmesan or Pecorino

Directions:
1. Preheat the air-fryer to 200°C/400°F.
2. Toss the broccoli in the oil, season with the garlic salt and pepper, then toss over the grated cheese and combine well. Add the broccoli to the preheated air-fryer and air-fry for 5 minutes, giving the broccoli a stir halfway through to ensure even cooking.

Cauliflower With Hot Sauce And Blue Cheese Sauce

Servings:2
Cooking Time:15 Minutes

Ingredients:
- For the cauliflower:
- 1 cauliflower, broken into florets
- 4 tbsp hot sauce
- 2 tbsp olive oil
- 1 tsp garlic powder
- ½ tsp salt
- ½ tsp black pepper
- 1 tbsp plain flour
- 1 tbsp corn starch
- For the blue cheese sauce:
- 50 g / 1.8 oz blue cheese, crumbled
- 2 tbsp sour cream
- 2 tbsp mayonnaise
- ½ tsp salt
- ½ tsp black pepper

Directions:
1. Preheat the air fryer to 180 °C / 350 °F and line the bottom of the basket with parchment paper.
2. In a bowl, combine the hot sauce, olive oil, garlic powder, salt, and black pepper until it forms a consistent mixture. Add the cauliflower to the bowl and coat in the sauce.
3. Stir in the plain flour and corn starch until well combined.
4. Transfer the cauliflower to the lined basket in the air fryer, close the lid, and cook for 12-15 minutes until the cauliflower has softened and is golden in colour.
5. Meanwhile, make the blue cheese sauce by combining all of the ingredients. When the cauliflower is ready, remove it from the air fryer and serve with the blue cheese sauce on the side.

Asparagus Spears

Servings: 2
Cooking Time:xx

Ingredients:
- 1 bunch of trimmed asparagus
- 1 teaspoon olive oil
- ¼ teaspoon salt
- ⅛ teaspoon freshly ground black pepper

Directions:
1. Preheat the air-fryer to 180ºC/350ºF.
2. Toss the asparagus spears in the oil and seasoning. Add these to the preheated air-fryer and air-fry for 8–12 minutes, turning once (cooking time depends on the thickness of the stalks, which should retain some bite).

Mediterranean Vegetables

Servings: 1–2
Cooking Time:xx

Ingredients:
- 1 courgette/zucchini, thickly sliced
- 1 (bell) pepper, deseeded and chopped into large chunks
- 1 red onion, sliced into wedges
- 12 cherry tomatoes
- 1 tablespoon olive oil
- ½ teaspoon salt
- ½ teaspoon freshly ground black pepper
- 2 rosemary twigs
- mozzarella, fresh pesto (see page 80) and basil leaves, to serve

Directions:
1. Preheat the air-fryer to 180ºC/350ºF.
2. Toss the prepared vegetables in the oil and seasoning. Add the vegetables and the rosemary to the preheated air-fryer and air-fry for 12–14 minutes, depending on how 'chargrilled' you like them.
3. Remove and serve topped with fresh mozzarella and pesto and scattered with basil leaves.

Crispy Cinnamon French Toast

Servings:2
Cooking Time:5 Minutes

Ingredients:
- 4 slices white bread
- 4 eggs
- 200 ml milk (cow's milk, cashew milk, soy milk, or oat milk)
- 2 tbsp granulated sugar
- 1 tsp brown sugar
- 1 tsp vanilla extract
- ½ tsp ground cinnamon

Directions:
1. Preheat your air fryer to 150 °C / 300 °F and line the bottom of the basket with parchment paper.
2. Cut each of the bread slices into 2 even rectangles and set them aside.
3. In a mixing bowl, whisk together the 4 eggs, milk, granulated sugar, brown sugar, vanilla extract, and ground cinnamon.
4. Soak the bread pieces in the egg mixture until they are fully covered and soaked in the mixture.
5. Place the coated bread slices in the lined air fryer, close the lid, and cook for 4-5 minutes until the bread is crispy and golden.
6. Serve the French toast slices with whatever toppings you desire.

Butternut Squash

Servings: 4
Cooking Time:xx

Ingredients:
- 500 g/1 lb. 2 oz. butternut squash, chopped into 2.5-cm/1-in. cubes
- 1 tablespoon olive oil or avocado oil
- 1 teaspoon smoked paprika
- 1 teaspoon dried oregano
- ½ teaspoon salt
- ¼ teaspoon freshly ground black pepper

Directions:
1. Preheat the air-fryer to 180ºC/350ºF.
2. In a bowl toss the butternut squash cubes in the oil and all the seasonings.
3. Add the butternut squash cubes to the preheated air-fryer and air-fry for 16–18 minutes, shaking the drawer once during cooking.

Garlic And Parsley Potatoes

Servings: 4
Cooking Time:xx

Ingredients:
- 500g baby potatoes, cut into quarters
- 1 tbsp oil
- 1 tsp salt
- ½ tsp garlic powder
- ½ tsp dried parsley

Directions:
1. Preheat air fryer to 175ºC
2. Combine potatoes and oil in a bowl
3. Add remaining ingredients and mix
4. Add to the air fryer and cook for about 25 minutes until golden brown, turning halfway through

Sweet And Sticky Parsnips And Carrots

Servings:2
Cooking Time:15 Minutes

Ingredients:
- 4 large carrots, peeled and chopped into long chunks
- 4 large parsnips, peeled and chopped into long chunks
- 1 tbsp olive oil
- 2 tbsp honey
- 1 tsp dried mixed herbs

Directions:
1. Preheat the air fryer to 150 °C / 300 °F and line the bottom of the basket with parchment paper.
2. Place the chopped carrots and parsnips in a large bowl and drizzle over the olive oil and honey. Sprinkle in some black pepper to taste and toss well to fully coat the vegetables.
3. Transfer the coated vegetables into the air fryer basket and shut the lid. Cook for 20 minutes until the carrots and parsnips and cooked and crispy.
4. Serve as a side with your dinner.

Butternut Squash Fries

Servings: 4
Cooking Time:xx

Ingredients:
- 400g butternut squash, cut into sticks
- 1 tbsp olive oil
- 2 tbsp bagel seasoning
- 1 tsp fresh chopped rosemary

Directions:
1. Preheat air fryer to 200ºC
2. Drizzle butternut squash with olive oil mix to coat
3. Add to the air fryer, cook for about 22 minutes until golden brown, stirring every 4 minutes
4. Sprinkle with bagel seasoning to serve

Celery Root Fries

Servings: 2
Cooking Time:xx

Ingredients:
- ½ celeriac, cut into sticks
- 500ml water
- 1 tbsp lime juice
- 1 tbsp olive oil
- 75g mayo
- 1 tbsp mustard
- 1 tbsp powdered horseradish

Directions:
1. Put celeriac in a bowl, add water and lime juice, soak for 30 minutes
2. Preheat air fryer to 200
3. Mix together the mayo, horseradish powder and mustard, refrigerate
4. Drain the celeriac, drizzle with oil and season with salt and pepper
5. Place in the air fryer and cook for about 10 minutes turning halfway
6. Serve with the mayo mix as a dip

Carrot & Parmesan Chips

Servings: 2
Cooking Time:xx

Ingredients:
- 180g carrots
- 1 tbsp olive oil
- 2 tbsp grated parmesan
- 1 crushed garlic clove
- Salt and pepper for seasoning

Directions:
1. Take a mixing bowl and add the olive oil and garlic, combining well
2. Remove the tops of the carrots and cut into halves, and then another half
3. Add the carrots to the bowl and toss well
4. Add the parmesan and coat the carrots well
5. Add the carrots to the air fryer and cook for 20 minutes at 220ºC, shaking halfway through

Yorkshire Puddings

Servings: 2
Cooking Time:xx

Ingredients:

- 1 tablespoon olive oil
- 70 g/½ cup plus ½ tablespoon plain/all-purpose flour (gluten-free if you wish)
- 100 ml/7 tablespoons milk
- 2 eggs
- salt and freshly ground black pepper

Directions:

1. You will need 4 ramekins. Preheat the air-fryer to 200ºC/400ºF.
2. Using a pastry brush, oil the base and sides of each ramekin, dividing the oil equally between the ramekins. Place the greased ramekins in the preheated air-fryer and heat for 5 minutes.
3. Meanwhile, in a food processor or using a whisk, combine the flour, milk, eggs and seasoning until you have a batter that is frothy on top. Divide the batter equally between the preheated ramekins. Return the ramekins to the air-fryer and air-fry for 20 minutes without opening the drawer. Remove the Yorkshire puddings from the ramekins and serve immediately.

Aubergine Parmesan

Servings: 4
Cooking Time:xx

Ingredients:

- 100g Italian breadcrumbs
- 50g grated parmesan
- 1 tsp Italian seasoning
- 1 tsp salt
- ½ tsp dried basil
- ½ tsp onion powder
- ½ tsp black pepper
- 100g flour
- 2 eggs
- 1 aubergine, sliced into ½ inch rounds

Directions:

1. Mix breadcrumbs, parmesan, salt Italian seasoning, basil, onion powder and pepper in a bowl
2. Add the flour to another bowl, and beat the eggs in another
3. Dip the aubergine in the flour, then the eggs and then coat in the bread crumbs
4. Preheat the air fryer to 185ºC
5. Place the aubergine in the air fryer and cook for 8-10 minutes
6. Turnover and cook for a further 4-6 minutes

Onion Rings

Servings: 4
Cooking Time:xx

Ingredients:
- 200g flour
- 75g cornstarch
- 2 tsp baking powder
- 1 tsp salt
- 2 pinches of paprika
- 1 large onion, cut into rings
- 1 egg
- 1 cup milk
- 200g breadcrumbs
- 2 pinches garlic powder

Directions:
1. Stir flour, salt, starch and baking powder together in a bowl
2. Dip onion rings into the flour mix to coat
3. Whisk the egg and milk into the flour mix, dip in the onion rings
4. Dip the onion rings into the bread crumbs
5. Heat the air fryer to 200ºC
6. Place the onion rings in the air fryer and cook for 2-3 minutes until golden brown
7. Sprinkle with paprika and garlic powder to serve

Grilled Bacon And Cheese

Servings: 2
Cooking Time:xx

Ingredients:
- 4 slices of regular bread
- 1 tbsp butter
- 2 slices cheddar cheese
- 5 slices bacon, pre-cooked
- 2 slices mozzarella cheese

Directions:
1. Place the butter into the microwave to melt
2. Spread the butter onto one side of the bread slices
3. Place one slice of bread into the fryer basket, with the buttered side facing downwards
4. Place the cheddar on top, followed by the bacon, mozzarella and the other slice of bread, with the buttered side facing upwards
5. Set your fryer to 170ºC and cook the sandwich for 4 minutes
6. Turn the sandwich over and cook for another 3 minutes
7. Turn the sandwich out and serve whilst hot
8. Repeat with the other remaining sandwich

Roasted Okra

Servings: 1
Cooking Time:xx

Ingredients:
- 300g Okra, ends trimmed and pods sliced
- 1 tsp olive oil
- ¼ tsp salt
- ⅛ tsp pepper

Directions:
1. Preheat the air fryer to 175ºC
2. Combine all ingredients in a bowl and stir gently
3. Place in the air fryer and cook for 5 minutes, shake and cook for another 5 minutes

Ranch-style Potatoes

Servings: 2
Cooking Time:xx

Ingredients:
- 300g baby potatoes, washed
- 1 tbsp olive oil
- 3 tbsp dry ranch seasoning

Directions:
1. Preheat the air fryer to 220ºC
2. Cut the potatoes in half
3. Take a mixing bowl and combine the olive oil with the ranch seasoning
4. Add the potatoes to the bowl and toss to coat
5. Cook for 15 minutes, shaking halfway through

Zingy Brussels Sprouts

Servings: 2
Cooking Time:xx

Ingredients:
- 1 tbsp avocado oil
- ½ tsp salt
- ½ tsp pepper
- 400g Brussels sprouts halved
- 1 tsp balsamic vinegar
- 2 tsp crumbled bacon

Directions:
1. Preheat air fryer to 175ºC
2. Combine oil, salt and pepper in a bowl and mix well. Add Brussels sprouts
3. Place in the air fryer and cook for 5 minutes shake then cook for another 5 minutes
4. Sprinkle with balsamic vinegar and sprinkle with bacon

Homemade Croquettes

Servings:4
Cooking Time:15 Minutes

Ingredients:

- 400 g / 14 oz white rice, uncooked
- 1 onion, sliced
- 2 cloves garlic, finely sliced
- 2 eggs, beaten
- 50 g / 3.5 oz parmesan cheese, grated
- 1 tsp salt
- 1 tsp black pepper
- 50 g / 3.5 oz breadcrumbs
- 1 tsp dried oregano

Directions:

1. In a large mixing bowl, combine the white rice, onion slices, garlic cloves slices, one beaten egg, parmesan cheese, and a sprinkle of salt and pepper.
2. Whisk the second egg in a separate bowl and place the breadcrumbs into another bowl.
3. Shape the mixture into 12 even croquettes and roll evenly in the egg, followed by the breadcrumbs.
4. Preheat the air fryer to 190 °C / 375 °F and line the bottom of the basket with parchment paper.
5. Place the croquettes in the lined air fryer basket and cook for 15 minutes, turning halfway through, until crispy and golden. Enjoy while hot as a side to your main dish.

Roasted Brussels Sprouts

Servings: 3
Cooking Time:xx

Ingredients:

- 300 g/10½ oz. Brussels sprouts, trimmed and halved
- 1 tablespoon olive oil
- ½ teaspoon salt
- ¼ teaspoon freshly ground black pepper

Directions:

1. Preheat the air-fryer to 160ºC/325ºF.
2. Toss the Brussels sprout halves in the oil and the seasoning. Add these to the preheated air-fryer and air-fry for 15 minutes, then increase the temperature of the air-fryer to 180ºC/350ºF and cook for a further 5 minutes until the sprouts are really crispy on the outside and cooked through.

Desserts Recipes

Shortbread Cookies

Servings: 2
Cooking Time:xx

Ingredients:

- 250g flour
- 75g sugar
- 175g butter
- 1 tbsp vanilla essence
- Chocolate buttons for decoration

Directions:

1. Preheat air fryer to 180°C
2. Place all ingredients apart from the chocolate into a bowl and rub together
3. Form into dough and roll out. Cut into heart shapes using a cookie cutter
4. Place in the air fryer and cook for 10 minutes
5. Place the chocolate buttons onto the shortbread and cook for another 10 minutes at 160°C

Blueberry Muffins

Servings: 12
Cooking Time:xx

Ingredients:

- 500g cups self raising flour
- 50g monk fruit
- 50g cream
- 225g oil
- 2 eggs
- 200g blueberries
- Zest and juice of 1 lemon
- 1 tbsp vanilla

Directions:

1. Mix together flour and sugar, set aside
2. In another bowl mix the remaining ingredients
3. Mix in the flour
4. Spoon the mix into silicone cupcake cases
5. Place in the air fryer and cook at 160°C for about 10 minutes

Cinnamon-maple Pineapple Kebabs

Servings: 2
Cooking Time:xx

Ingredients:

- 4 x pineapple strips, roughly 2 x 2 cm/¾ x ¾ in. by length of pineapple
- 1 teaspoon maple syrup
- ½ teaspoon vanilla extract
- ¼ teaspoon ground cinnamon
- Greek or plant-based yogurt and grated lime zest, to serve

Directions:

1. Line the air-fryer with an air-fryer liner or a piece of pierced parchment paper. Preheat the air-fryer to 180°C/350°F.
2. Stick small metal skewers through the pineapple lengthways. Mix the maple syrup and vanilla extract together, then drizzle over the pineapple and sprinkle over the cinnamon.
3. Add the skewers to the preheated lined air-fryer and air-fry for 15 minutes, turning once. If there is any maple-vanilla mixture left after the initial drizzle, then drizzle this over the pineapple during cooking too. Serve with yogurt and lime zest.

New York Cheesecake

Servings: 8
Cooking Time:xx

Ingredients:

- 225g plain flour
- 100g brown sugar
- 100g butter
- 50g melted butter
- 1 tbsp vanilla essence
- 750g soft cheese
- 2 cups caster sugar
- 3 large eggs
- 50ml quark

Directions:

1. Add the flour, sugar, and 100g butter to a bowl and mix until combined. Form into biscuit shapes place in the air fryer and cook for 15 minutes at 180°C
2. Grease a springform tin
3. Break the biscuits up and mix with the melted butter, press firmly into the tin
4. Mix the soft cheese and sugar in a bowl until creamy, add the eggs and vanilla and mix. Mix in the quark
5. Pour the cheesecake batter into the pan
6. Place in your air fryer and cook for 30 minutes at 180°C. Leave in the air fryer for 30 minutes whilst it cools
7. Refrigerate for 6 hours

Granola Bars

Servings: 6
Cooking Time:xx

Ingredients:

- 250g oats
- 60g melted butter
- 30g sugar
- 3 tbsp honey
- Handful of raisins
- 1 apple cooked and peeled
- 1 tbsp olive oil
- 1 tsp vanilla
- 1 tsp cinnamon

Directions:

1. Add all the dry ingredients to the blender and mix
2. Add all the wet ingredients to the air fryer pan and mix well
3. Add the dry ingredients and mix well
4. Add the raisins and press down the mix into the pan
5. Cook for 10 mins at 160°C then at 5 minutes for 180°C
6. Chop into bars and serve

Pop Tarts

Servings: 6
Cooking Time:xx

Ingredients:

- 200g strawberries quartered
- 25g sugar
- ½ pack ready made pie crust
- Cooking spray
- 50g powdered sugar
- 1 ½ tsp lemon juice
- 1 tbsp sprinkles

Directions:

1. Stir together strawberries and sugar in a bowl
2. Allow to stand for 15 minutes then microwave on high for 10 minutes stirring halfway through
3. Roll out pie crust int0 12 inch circle, cut into 12 rectangles
4. Spoon mix onto 6 of the rectangles
5. Brush the edges with water and top with the remaining rectangles
6. Press around the edges with a fork to seal
7. Place in the air fryer and cook at 175ºC for about 10 minutes
8. Mix together powdered sugar and decorate add sprinkles

Apple And Cinnamon Empanadas

Servings: 12
Cooking Time:xx

Ingredients:

- 12 empanada wraps
- 2 diced apples
- 2 tbsp honey
- 1 tsp vanilla extract
- 1 tsp cinnamon
- ⅛ tsp nutmeg
- Olive oil spray
- 2 tsp cornstarch
- 1 tsp water

Directions:

1. Place apples, cinnamon, honey, vanilla and nutmeg in a pan cook for 2-3 minutes until apples are soft
2. Mix the cornstarch and water add to the pan and cook for 30 seconds
3. Add the apple mix to each of the empanada wraps
4. Roll the wrap in half, pinch along the edges, fold the edges in then continue to roll to seal
5. Place in the air fryer and cook at 200ºC for 8 minutes, turn and cook for another 10 minutes

Fruit Crumble

Servings: 2
Cooking Time:xx

Ingredients:
- 1 diced apple
- 75g frozen blackberries
- 25g brown rice flour
- 2 tbsp sugar
- ½ tsp cinnamon
- 2 tbsp butter

Directions:
1. Preheat air fryer to 150ºC
2. Mix apple and blackberries in an air fryer safe baking pan
3. In a bowl mix the flour, sugar, cinnamon and butter, spoon over the fruit
4. Cook for 15 minutes

Chocolate Dipped Biscuits

Servings: 6
Cooking Time:xx

Ingredients:
- 225g self raising flour
- 100g sugar
- 100g butter
- 50g milk chocolate
- 1 egg beaten
- 1 tsp vanilla essence

Directions:
1. Add the flour, butter and sugar to a bowl and rub together
2. Add the egg and vanilla, mix to form a dough
3. Split the dough into 6 and form into balls
4. Place in the air fryer cook at 180ºC for 15 minutes
5. Melt the chocolate, dip the cooked biscuits into the chocolate and half cover

Pecan & Molasses Flapjack

Servings:9
Cooking Time:xx

Ingredients:
- 120 g/½ cup plus 2 teaspoons butter or plant-based spread, plus extra for greasing
- 40 g/2 tablespoons blackstrap molasses
- 60 g/5 tablespoons unrefined sugar
- 50 g/½ cup chopped pecans
- 200 g/1½ cups porridge oats/steelcut oats (not rolled or jumbo)

Directions:
1. Preheat the air-fryer to 180ºC/350ºF.
2. Grease and line a 15 x 15-cm/6 x 6-in. baking pan.
3. In a large saucepan melt the butter/spread, molasses and sugar. Once melted, stir in the pecans, then the oats. As soon as they are combined, tip the mixture into the prepared baking pan and cover with foil.
4. Place the foil-covered baking pan in the preheated air-fryer and air-fry for 10 minutes. Remove the foil, then cook for a further 2 minutes to brown the top. Leave to cool, then cut into 9 squares.

S'mores

Servings: 2
Cooking Time:xx

Ingredients:

- 2 graham crackers, broken in half
- 2 marshmallows, halved
- 2 pieces of chocolate

Directions:

1. Place 2 halves of graham crackers in the air fryer and add a marshmallow to each sticky side down
2. Cook in the air fryer at 180ºC for 5 minutes until the marshmallows are golden
3. Remove from the air fryer add a piece of chocolate and top with the other half of graham crackers

Apple And Cinnamon Puff Pastry Pies

Servings:8
Cooking Time:20 Minutes

Ingredients:

- 4 tbsp butter
- 4 tbsp white sugar
- 2 tbsp brown sugar
- 1 tsp cinnamon
- 1 tsp nutmeg
- 1 tsp salt
- 4 apples, peeled and diced
- 2 large sheets puff pastry
- 1 egg

Directions:

1. Preheat the air fryer to 180 °C / 350 °F. Remove the mesh basket from the machine and line it with parchment paper.
2. In a bowl, whisk together the butter, white sugar, brown sugar, cinnamon, nutmeg, and salt.
3. Place the apples in a heatproof baking dish and coat them in the butter and sugar mixture. Transfer to the air fryer and cook for 10 minutes.
4. Meanwhile, roll out the pastry on a clean, floured surface. Cut the sheets into 8 equal parts.
5. Once the apples are hot and softened, evenly spread the mixture between the pastry sheets. Fold the sheets over to cover the apple and gently press the edges using a fork or your fingers to seal the mixture in.
6. Beat the egg in a bowl and use a brush to coat the top of each pastry sheet.
7. Carefully transfer the filled pastry sheets to the prepared air fryer basket, close the lid, and cook for 10 minutes until the pastry is golden and crispy.

Tasty Cannoli

Servings: 4
Cooking Time:xx

Ingredients:

- 400g ricotta cheese
- 200g mascarpone cheese
- 150g icing sugar
- 160ml double cream
- 1 tsp vanilla extract
- 1 tsp orange zest
- 150g mini chocolate chips
- 350g flour
- 150g sugar
- 1 tsp salt
- 1/2 tsp cinnamon
- 6 tbsp white wine
- 1 egg, plus 1 extra egg white
- 4 tbsp cubed cold butter

Directions:

1. Take a large mixing bowl and a hand mixer. Combine the cream and half the icing sugar until you see stiff peaks starting to form
2. Take another bowl and combine the rest of the icing sugar with the ricotta, mascarpone, zest, salt and vanilla
3. Fold the ricotta mixture into the cream mixture carefully and place in the refrigerator for 1 hour
4. Take a large bowl and combine the cinnamon, salt, sugar and lour
5. Cut the butter into chunks and add to the mixture, combining well
6. Add the egg and the wine and combine until you see a dough starting to form
7. Cover the dough with plastic wrap and place in the refrigerator for 1 hour
8. Cut the dough into halves and roll each half into about 1/8" thickness
9. Use a cookie cutter (around 4" size) to cut out rounds
10. Wrap the cold dough around your cannoli moulds
11. Brush the seal with the egg white to hold it together
12. Preheat the air fryer to 220°C
13. Place the cannoli in the basket and cook for 12 minutes
14. Once cooled slightly, remove the moulds
15. Place the cream mixture into a pastry bag and pipe into the cannoli shells
16. Dip both ends into the chocolate chips for decoration

Chocolate Mug Cake

Servings: 1
Cooking Time:xx

Ingredients:

- 30g self raising flour
- 5 tbsp sugar
- 1 tbsp cocoa powder
- 3 tbsp milk
- 3 tsp coconut oil

Directions:

1. Mix all the ingredients together in a mug
2. Heat the air fryer to 200°C
3. Place the mug in the air fryer and cook for 10 minutes

Cinnamon Biscuit Bites

Servings: 16
Cooking Time:xx

Ingredients:
- 200g flour
- 200g wholewheat flour
- 2 tbsp sugar
- 1 tsp baking powder
- ¼ tsp cinnamon
- ¼ tsp salt
- 4 tbsp butter
- 50ml milk
- Cooking spray
- 300g icing sugar
- 3 tbsp water

Directions:
1. Mix together flour, salt, sugar baking powder and cinnamon in a bowl
2. Add butter and mix until well combined
3. Add milk and form a dough, place dough on a floured surface and knead until smooth
4. Cut into 16 equal pieces and form each piece into a ball
5. Place in the air fryer and cook at 180ºC for about 12 minutes
6. Mix together icing sugar and water and coat to serve

Apple Pie

Servings: 2
Cooking Time:xx

Ingredients:
- 1 packet of ready made pastry
- 1 apple, chopped
- 2 tsp lemon juice
- 1 tsp cinnamon
- 2 tbsp sugar
- ½ tsp vanilla extract
- 1 tbsp butter
- 1 beaten egg
- 1 tbsp raw sugar

Directions:
1. Preheat the air fryer to 160ºC
2. Line a baking tin with pastry
3. Mix the apple, lemon juice, cinnamon, sugar and vanilla in a bowl
4. Pour the apple mix into the tin with the pastry, top with chunks of butter
5. Cover with a second piece of pastry, place three slits in the top of the pastry
6. Brush the pastry with beaten egg and sprinkle with raw sugar
7. Place in the air fryer and cook for 30 minutes

Breakfast Muffins

Servings:4
Cooking Time:xx

Ingredients:

- 1 eating apple, cored and grated
- 40 g/2 heaped tablespoons maple syrup
- 40 ml/3 tablespoons oil (avocado, olive or coconut), plus extra for greasing
- 1 egg
- 40 ml/3 tablespoons milk (plant-based if you wish)
- 90 g/scant ¾ cup brown rice flour
- 50 g/½ cup ground almonds
- ¾ teaspoon ground cinnamon
- ⅛ teaspoon ground cloves
- ¼ teaspoon salt
- 1 teaspoon baking powder
- Greek or plant-based yogurt and fresh fruit, to serve

Directions:

1. In a bowl mix the grated apple, maple syrup, oil, egg and milk. In another bowl mix the rice flour, ground almonds, cinnamon, cloves, salt and baking powder. Combine the wet ingredients with the dry, mixing until there are no visible patches of the flour mixture left. Grease 4 ramekins and divide the batter equally between them.
2. Preheat the air-fryer to 160°C/325°F.
3. Add the ramekins to the preheated air-fryer and air-fry for 12 minutes. Check the muffins are cooked by inserting a cocktail stick/toothpick into the middle of one of the muffins. If it comes out clean, the muffins are ready; if not, cook for a further couple of minutes.
4. Allow to cool in the ramekins, then remove and serve with your choice of yogurt and fresh fruit.

Granola

Servings: 3
Cooking Time:xx

Ingredients:

- 60 g/¼ cup runny honey
- 50 g/3 tablespoons coconut oil
- 1 teaspoon vanilla extract
- 100 g/¾ cup jumbo rolled oats/old-fashioned oats (not porridge oats)
- 50 g/½ cup chopped walnuts
- 1 teaspoon ground cinnamon

Directions:

1. Preheat the air-fryer to 180°C/350°F.
2. Place the honey, coconut oil and vanilla extract in a small dish. Add this to the preheated air-fryer for 1 minute to melt.
3. In a small bowl combine the oats, nuts and cinnamon. Add the melted honey mixture and toss well, ensuring all the oats and nuts are well coated.
4. Lay an air-fryer liner or a pierced piece of parchment paper on the base of the air-fryer drawer. Add the granola mix on top, spread evenly in one layer. Air-fry for 4 minutes, then stir before cooking for a further 3 minutes. Leave to cool completely before serving or storing in a jar.

Chocolate And Berry Pop Tarts

Servings:8
Cooking Time:10 Minutes

Ingredients:
- For the filling:
- 50 g / 1.8 oz fresh raspberries
- 50 g / 1.8 oz fresh strawberries
- 100 g / 3.5 oz granulated sugar
- 1 tsp corn starch
- For the pastry:
- 1 sheet puff pastry
- For the frosting:
- 4 tbsp powdered sugar
- 2 tbsp maple syrup or honey
- Chocolate sprinkles

Directions:
1. Preheat the air fryer to 180 °C / 350 °F and line the mesh basket with parchment paper or grease it with olive oil.
2. Make the filling by combining the strawberries, raspberries, and granulated sugar in a saucepan. Place on medium heat until the mixture starts to boil. When it begins to boil, turn the temperature down to a low setting. Use a spoon to break up the berries and forms a smooth mixture.
3. Stir in the corn starch and let the mixture simmer for 1-2 minutes. Remove the saucepan from the heat and set aside to cool while you prepare the pastry.
4. Roll out the large sheet of puff pastry and cut it into 8 equal rectangles.
5. Spoon 2 tbsp of the cooled berry filling onto one side of each rectangle. Fold over the other side of each puff pastry rectangle to cover the filling. Press the sides down with a fork or using your fingers to seal the filling into the pastry.
6. Transfer the puff pastry rectangles into the lined air fryer basket. Cook for 10-12 minutes until the pastry is golden and crispy.
7. Meanwhile, make the frosting. Whisk together the powdered sugar, maple syrup or honey, and chocolate chips in a bowl until well combined.
8. Carefully spread a thin layer of frosting in the centre of each pop tart. Allow the frosting to set before serving.

Apple Fritters

Servings: 4
Cooking Time:xx

Ingredients:
- 225g self raising flour
- 200g greek yogurt
- 2 tsp sugar
- 1 tbsp cinnamon
- 1 apple peeled and chopped
- 225g icing sugar
- 2 tbsp milk

Directions:
1. Mix the flour, yogurt, sugar, cinnamon and apple together. Knead for about 3 -4 minutes
2. Mix the icing sugar and milk together to make the glaze and set aside
3. Line the air fryer with parchment paper and spray with cooking spray
4. Divide the fritter mix into four, flatten each portion and place in the air fryer
5. Cook at 185ºC for about 15 minutes turning halfway
6. Drizzle with glaze to serve

Appendix : Recipes Index

A

Air Fried Scallops 61
Air Fryer Cheese Sandwich 66
Air Fryer Chicken Thigh Schnitzel 31
Air-fried Artichoke Hearts 66
Air-fried Pickles 29
Apple And Cinnamon Empanadas 85
Apple And Cinnamon Puff Pastry Pies 87
Apple Fritters 91
Apple Pie 89
Artichoke Crostini 70
Artichoke Pasta 71
Asian Devilled Eggs 25
Asparagus & Steak Parcels 46
Asparagus Spears 75
Aubergine Parmesan 78
Aubergine Parmigiana 72
Avocado Fries 18

B

Baked Aubergine Slices With Yogurt Dressing 69
Baked Feta, Tomato & Garlic Pasta 67
Beef Bulgogi Burgers 46
Beef Satay 43
Blueberry Muffins 83
Bocconcini Balls 19
Breakfast Muffins 90
Buffalo Wings 32
Butternut Squash Fries 77
Butternut Squash 76

C

Carrot & Parmesan Chips 77
Cauliflower With Hot Sauce And Blue Cheese Sauce 74
Celery Root Fries 77
Charred Chicken Breasts 35
Cheese Wontons 24
Cheesy Meatballs 48
Chicken & Bacon Parcels 25
Chicken & Potatoes 40
Chicken And Cheese Chimichangas 37
Chicken Fried Rice 36
Chicken Kiev 38
Chicken Milanese 31
Chicken Parmesan With Marinara Sauce 34
Chicken Tikka Masala 34
Chocolate And Berry Pop Tarts 91
Chocolate Dipped Biscuits 86
Chocolate Mug Cake 88
Cinnamon Biscuit Bites 89
Cinnamon-maple Pineapple Kebabs 83
Cod Nuggets 58
Copycat Fish Fingers 59
Corn Nuts 28
Courgette Fries 14
Courgette Meatballs 63
Crispy Broccoli 74
Crispy Cinnamon French Toast 75
Crispy Nacho Prawns 54
Crispy Potato Peels 72
Crunchy Fish 57

E

Easy Cheese & Bacon Toasties 19
European Pancakes 17

F

Falafel Burgers 71
Fish In Foil 58
Fish In Parchment Paper 56
Fish Taco Cauliflower Rice Bowls 57
French Toast Slices 13
Fruit Crumble 86

G

Garlic And Parsley Potatoes 76
Garlic Butter Salmon 58
Garlic Pizza Toast 22
Garlic Tilapia 55
Granola Bars 84
Granola 90
Grilled Bacon And Cheese 79

H

Hamburgers 51
Hard Boiled Eggs Air Fryer Style 15
Healthy Bang Bang Chicken 33
Homemade Croquettes 81
Honey Cajun Chicken Thighs 39
Honey Sriracha Salmon 54

I

Italian Rice Balls 29

L

Lobster Tails 53
Lumpia 27

M

Mac & Cheese Bites 22
Macaroni & Cheese Quiche 68
Maine Seafood 59
Meatballs In Tomato Sauce 47
Mediterranean Vegetables 75
Mexican Breakfast Burritos 18
Mini Calzones 22
Mini Quiche 68
Monte Cristo Breakfast Sandwich 14
Muhammara 15

N

Nashville Chicken 36
New York Cheesecake 84

O

Oat & Parmesan Crusted Fish Fillets 61
Old Fashioned Steak 42
Olive Stained Turkey Breast 33
Onion Bahji 24
Onion Pakoda 28
Onion Rings 79
Oozing Baked Eggs 13
Orange Chicken 40

P

Parmesan Crusted Pork Chops 50
Parmesan-coated Fish Fingers 53
Pasta Chips 23
Pecan & Molasses Flapjack 86
Pepper & Lemon Chicken Wings 37
Pitta Pizza 17
Pizza Chicken Nuggets 35
Pizza Dogs 44
Plantain Fries 13
Polenta Fries 12
Pop Tarts 85
Popcorn Tofu 21
Pork Chilli Cheese Dogs 50
Pork Chops With Honey 49
Pork Chops With Raspberry And Balsamic 51
Pork Schnitzel 48
Pork Taquitos 44
Potato & Chorizo Frittata 16
Pulled Pork, Bacon, And Cheese Sliders 45

Q

Quick Chicken Nuggets 39

R

Ranch-style Potatoes 80
Raspberry Breakfast Pockets 16
Ratatouille 64
Roast Beef 42
Roasted Brussels Sprouts 81
Roasted Okra 80
Roasted Vegetable Pasta 69

S

S'mores 87
Satay Tofu Skewers 67
Sausage Burritos 47
Shortbread Cookies 83
Shrimp With Yum Yum Sauce 54
Shrimp Wrapped With Bacon 60
Snack Style Falafel 21
Store-cupboard Fishcakes 55
Stuffed Mushrooms 26
Stuffed Peppers 65
Swede Fries 12
Sweet And Sticky Parsnips And Carrots 76

T

Taco Lasagne Pie 45
Tahini Beef Bites 43
Tangy Breakfast Hash 15
Tasty Cannoli 88
Tasty Pumpkin Seeds 26
Tender Ham Steaks 49
Thai Bites 23
Thai Salmon Patties 60
Thai Turkey Burgers 32
Tortellini Bites 27
Traditional Fish And Chips 56
Turkey Cutlets In Mushroom Sauce 38
Two-step Pizza 64

V

Vegan Fried Ravioli 70
Vegetarian "chicken" Tenders 65
Veggie Lasagne 63

W

Waffle Fries 26
Wholegrain Pitta Chips 17

Y

Yorkshire Puddings 78
Your Favourite Breakfast Bacon 19

Z

Zingy Brussels Sprouts 80

Printed in Great Britain
by Amazon

22443673R00057